A POCKET GUIDE TO
RISK MATHEMATICS

A POCKET GUIDE TO RISK MATHEMATICS

Key Concepts Every Auditor Should Know

MATTHEW LEITCH

A John Wiley and Sons, Ltd, Publication

This edition first published 2010 by John Wiley & Sons, Ltd
Copyright © 2010 Matthew Leitch

Registered office
John Wiley & Sons Ltd, The Atrium, Southern Gate, Chichester, West Sussex, PO19 8SQ, United Kingdom

For details of our global editorial offices, for customer services and for information about how to apply for permission to reuse the copyright material in this book please see our website at www.wiley.com.

The right of the author to be identified as the author of this work has been asserted in accordance with the Copyright, Designs and Patents Act 1988.

Wiley also publishes its books in a variety of electronic formats. Some content that appears in print may not be available in electronic books.

Designations used by companies to distinguish their products are often claimed as trademarks. All brand names and product names used in this book are trade names, service marks, trademarks or registered trademarks of their respective owners. The publisher is not associated with any product or vendor mentioned in this book. This publication is designed to provide accurate and authoritative information in regard to the subject matter covered. It is sold on the understanding that the publisher is not engaged in rendering professional services. If professional advice or other expert assistance is required, the services of a competent professional should be sought.

ISBN 978-0-470-71052-4

A catalogue record for this book is available from the British Library.

Set in 10/12pt Garamond Pro by Sparks – www.sparkspublishing.com
Printed in Great Britain by TJ International Ltd, Padstow, Cornwall

CONTENTS

START HERE

Good choice!

This book is designed to do one job very well. If you read it as it is designed to be read, step by step, from start to finish, it will *transform* your understanding of risk and the mathematics involved, and will give you the confidence to tackle audits that would have been out of reach without it.

The book makes this possible by taking the pain out of the subject. Instead of bombarding you with symbols and formulae, it explains the ideas involved using mainly words and pictures so that you can understand it. In this way the book covers many more topics than a traditional mathematical textbook of the same size.

The book also focuses on the real needs of auditors. Auditors do not need to be able to do something themselves to audit it. They just need to understand the subject, know what problems to look for, and have some ideas about what to suggest. Ideally, their knowledge will be deep without necessarily being detailed. This book gives you those insights, without demanding that you spend months doing calculus.

Among other things, this book explains mathematical techniques that lead to systematic understatement of risk, so that you can suggest either changes in approach or better disclosure of the limitations of risk numbers. Some of these techniques are so simple and familiar they hardly deserve to be called mathematical, while others are more involved.

This is good for you and for your employer or clients, but it's more than that. It's good for society as a whole. Risk is a big issue these days, with important decisions influenced by assessments of risk ranging from gut feelings to the numbers produced by sophisticated computerized simulations. Overconfident reliance on these numbers can lead to lost lives and lost livelihoods, as the billions lost by banks during the 2007–2009 credit crunch showed.

Auditors need to play their part in stopping this from happening and, indeed, for years the audit profession, internal and external, has been positioning itself as a source of risk-focused assurance. It's been saying that auditors are experts in risk – and so we are, in a sense – but what about the fundamental logic of risk? The truth is that most of us feel a bit uneasy about risk *mathematics*.

Most likely you learned some of the mathematics involved at school or university, but your knowledge is a bit rusty. If someone mentions 'normal distribution' you sort of know what that is, but vaguely.

And that's a problem because some very big mistakes have been made by organizations that analysed risk badly, with no concerns raised by their auditors. I'm not talking about making a slip in the calculus, or going wrong somewhere in the algebra. The mistakes were big, conceptual mistakes that auditors could have understood and pointed out.

And things can get into an embarrassing muddle when it's the auditors themselves doing the risk analysis. It's not uncommon to see risk analyses done by auditors, or with their advice, that are let down by elementary mathematical errors.

This book

This book has been designed as the quickest, easiest, most convenient solution to that problem ever written.

Only the key concepts are explained, and always by building on ideas already covered. The emphasis is on having a confident, conceptual understanding and the ability to spot mistakes – a large number of which are explained and highlighted.

Obviously, reading this book requires time and effort, it's not a comprehensive guide to risk mathematics and its mistakes, and you still won't be able to do the mathematics yourself. However, this book is so much easier than the traditional alternatives that it changes what auditors can do, fundamentally.

While travelling to work perhaps, spend 20 minutes a day for as long as it takes to read through this book and your expertise will be transformed. Your audit colleagues will be staggered by your knowledge, and interesting reviews with risk at their core will be yours to choose.

And when a risk quant (i.e. risk mathematician) tries to blind you with technicalities you can smoothly reply with something like, 'I see your point about the Gaussians, but you still haven't explained your approach to model uncertainty.' Imagine the blood draining from the face of your unsuspecting tormentor.

Not sure you want to make the investment? Give it a try and you'll be amazed at the *practical* importance of the stuff you didn't know.

How this book works

Filling your mind with the basic concepts and terminology of a discipline is the fastest way to start becoming an expert and a great way to become a good amateur. That's why this book is made up of small, digestible chunks, each focusing on an idea and its terminology.

Many years ago I had to make myself an expert in telecommunication businesses and to get started I bought a book called *Pocket Telecommunications* that had alphabetically ordered entries explaining industry jargon. I read it every day on my train journeys to and from work. After about two weeks I had finished the little book and I felt different. I was different. I could read books and articles about the industry and understand what they meant. I could talk to people with years of telecommunications experience and get away with it.

Most amazing of all was that I found I was more of an expert than most people I worked with, many of whom were supposed to have years of industry experience behind them. It's astonishing what a little homework can achieve when it is focused on the right things.

This book is designed to help you transform yourself in that way. It introduces a series of ideas and terms about the mathematics of risk.

It builds them up systematically, starting with things you will already know and teaching you what you need to understand in order to go further. All the terms have been analysed to find the dependencies and make sure you are not blocked by explanations that make no sense.

As far as possible I've used plain English and kept formulae to a minimum. The examples are simple ones because it is concepts that you need to understand most.

The ideas are grouped by topic, and there's an alphabetical index too. Each idea is identified by a word or phrase and where that is used in the text it is **in bold** to remind you to think of its technical meaning.

To keep you motivated the book is littered with 'audit points' – specific issues to look for and ideas for what to recommend. There are also opportunities to test how your knowledge is growing, chapter by chapter, item by item.

In writing this book I consulted several mathematical dictionaries and many other sources, and of course they didn't agree with each other. I've tried to select definitions that are logical, easy to understand, and easy to define without lengthy theoretical groundwork.

In a few cases I've had to invent suitable terminology to label ideas that don't have an established name.

You should read a bit of the book every day, starting at the beginning and reading carefully. If you're not sure about a section then read it again, but it's not necessary for you to understand every point to gain a huge boost in confidence and competence.

Every new idea you absorb will raise your ability to understand and critically appraise risk mathematics you read. You may even find you have knowledge that some professional quants lack, perhaps because they have focused on the mechanics of what they do and not had time to look around at the bigger picture.

When you've finished the book it will be time to test yourself by trying to read documents about risk mathematics, preferably from inside your own organization. See how much more you can understand, at least in principle, from the text. (You won't be much better at understanding the formulae.)

This is a vast subject area, so there will still be lots that you don't recognize. Gradually you will get better at spotting where people are using terms incorrectly, or have not explained something they should have, and you will be tripped up by fewer details.

Be sensible about which audits you can take on using your new powers. Auditing key pricing models constructed by leading mathematicians is still likely to be out of your reach. If mathematicians try hard to cover up the weaknesses in their work you may struggle. And it still won't be sensible to try to check the algebra or computer code yourself.

However, everyday risk assessments by non-specialists will look very different to you and they will be an easy target. Somewhat quantitative risk work by pseudo-mathematicians who barely understand what they are doing will also be your happy hunting ground. And when the big models are reviewed by quant review teams you will understand far more of what their review covered and what it did not and perhaps should have.

The myth of mathematical clarity

Mathematics does something quite brilliant. By reducing ideas to small, easy-to-write symbols it makes it possible to say a lot in a small area. Manipulating the ideas becomes dramatically easier, making possible deductions that would be desperately tiring and slow using words alone.

Mathematical thinking about risk and uncertainty is far ahead of the muddle that most of us have in our heads. Understanding its fundamentals will make many things clear to you, perhaps for the first time.

However, it's a myth that mathematics is clear. A lot of mathematical writing is diabolical. Never assume you can't understand some mathematics because you are ignorant or stupid. It's very likely that the main reason you can't understand, even after a sincere effort, is that it is written poorly.

Common problems include misleading terms, lack of type declarations (introducing a symbol without even saying what kind of thing it is), assuming the reader already knows what the writer is trying to say, using the same notation to mean different things, and using obscure letters from the ancient Greek alphabet that many people cannot name. Do you know what η is? Me neither, I had to look it up. (It's eta.)

A great deal is usually left to the reader to know from the context, as if by magic. (Mathematics that is written to be checked by a computer program has to be written very differently.)

All this is harder still if the writer's command of English is weak and the format is PowerPoint.

Another reason that mathematical writing is often confusing is that mathematics changes over time. New ways of doing things, new terminology, and new notation get invented and gradually permeate the literature. So what we see today is a mixture of ideas and styles from different eras.

Finally, and perhaps most importantly, mathematics uses many ordinary, familiar words but in very specific and unfamiliar ways. The scope for misunderstandings in everyday situations is frightening.

For example, imagine a room full of managers being told that 'the *expected value* of this project is £3.2 million.' Many of those managers will think this means that the project will deliver £3.2 million (perhaps give or take a few thousand) and that this is more likely to happen than not. In ordinary language that's what 'expected' means in this context. What the speaker actually meant was that the project's value is unknown but the probability weighted average of his guesses so far is £3.2 million. I hope you can see that there's a big difference!

So, never assume that not understanding some mathematical document is your fault. Make a sincere and patient effort to understand written mathematics. Reread the text. Be wary even of familiar words and phrases. Look carefully for things that are not made clear and identify them specifically.

Then ask, just as if it was any other audit. You are entitled to a clear explanation and if someone cannot give it then *their* understanding must be doubted.

The myths of quantification

Understandably, many people think a mathematical approach to risk necessarily means a quantitative approach, and that a quantitative approach must have data to support it. It is true that in some famous applications of mathematics to risk (in financial markets and weather forecasting, for example) the approach is quantitative and supported by massive amounts of data. It is also true that mathematical risk analysis is at its best when quantified and supported by data.

However, it is not true that mathematics is restricted to quantitative analysis, and not true that it must have plentiful data.

Mathematics is a commitment to logical thinking. It can help us squeeze the most learning from limited data. If the only data we have are our gut feelings it can help us make best use of them. Given things we are confident we can guesstimate, it can be used to calculate things that defy intuition. It can show us where our gut feelings are logically inconsistent and could lead to us losing money.

The essence of the mathematical approach to risk is not quantification or data, but something much simpler and more familiar. It is building a model of a problem, and recognizing uncertainty around that model. You may have experienced this centuries-old method at school when tackling the topic of probability, or on a business course, or while studying for an accountancy qualification. Your thinking encompassed the whole problem or system, with 'risk' recognized in the form of uncertainties about values in the model, usually shown using probabilities.

Contrast this with the language and procedures of 'risk management' as it has sprung up over just the last few decades, where 'risks' are talked of as if they are physical phenomena, out there, to be found and listed, unrelated to other thinking. This perspective inevitably leads to 'risk' being separated from other management activities, with separate risk management meetings, risk reports, risk teams, and so on – all cut off from the main action of management.

A mathematical approach is a step forward from this, even without quantification or data.

The auditor's mission

What is the auditor's mission in auditing risk assessments and models? There's plenty to go for.

Over-reliance on flawed (usually optimistic) risk assessments has led to innumerable failed projects and other business ventures, and was at the heart of the 2007–2009 credit crunch. Obviously we'd like to spot the mistakes before they can cause damage, if we can, and recommend better practices to use in future.

To be successful in this there is one thing auditors should focus on above all else when reviewing risk assessments: our human tendency to underestimate and ignore our uncertainty.

This is such a powerful syndrome of behaviours, and so universal, that it seems at times like a vast conspiracy.

The risk analyst wants to make assumptions that are easy to work with and wants to present results that seem precise and trustworthy. He sees no need to go on about the many simplifying assumptions made, or the flawed data used, or the dangers of extrapolating into the future. Why should he when his audience, managers, so often appear not to want to hear that kind of material? They want numbers that will support the actions they already want to take.

Similarly, the analyst sees no need to mention the bits of his own work he doesn't fully understand, or the bits he knows to be wrong in small and probably insignificant ways. (Or so he thinks.) Why should he when nobody else knows enough to find him out?

Enter the auditor. Already secretly fearing that the conversation will quickly get confusing, the auditor dives for the easy tests he can understand. Were the documents signed off by people in authority? Have they been reviewed by someone with experience and credentials? Was the data used taken from a computer system that's already been audited? (Thinking: 'Crikey, did he just say "general linear model" and is a "Kalman filter" something else in the model or an invitation to take a coffee break? It's time to finish this meeting and get out of here.')

It doesn't have to be this way. With a bit of knowledge and reassurance it should be like any other audit of something the experts know better than the auditor. Ask questions, listen carefully, don't be afraid to probe, make an effort to grasp the issues, and close in when people get defensive.

Time and again you will find that what people have done has led to a misstatement of risk, usually an understatement. Consequently, risk is not being taken as seriously as it should be. If you can get the risk analysed or presented more fairly then you can change how people respond to it and perhaps prevent some of the disasters of the past from happening again.

AUDITING SIMPLE RISK ASSESSMENTS

This chapter introduces the most basic ideas of probability and risk and shows how they can help us audit simple risk assessments.

These are the sort of casual risk assessments that pop up in conversation and on risk registers. Even at this simple level you will find a lot of surprises and helpful insights.

To start with, in the world of business, 'risk' has a high profile and 'probability' is a word a lot of people try to avoid. In the world of mathematics the situation is reversed, with 'probability' the undisputed king and 'risk' an afterthought, sneaking in from theories about investment portfolios.

As you read on, remember how this book is designed. It's a series of concepts and terms, each of which will help you in your work. Tackle them in order, patiently and carefully. Your objective is to learn as much as you can, not to finish the book as quickly as possible.

1   PROBABILITIES

A lot of ideas about **probabilities** are controversial among theorists or take a while to understand, but what we know for certain is that probabilities *work*. There are people who talk about and benefit from using **probabilities** and this has been true for hundreds of years.

One of the great pioneers of the mathematics of **probability** was Frenchman Pierre-Simon Laplace (1749–1827). In the introduction to his book, *Théorie Analytique des Probabilités*, he wrote that 'que la théorie des probabilités n'est, au fond, que le bon sens réduit au calcul,' which means 'the theory of probability is just common sense reduced to calculation.'

what we know for certain is that probabilities work

Probabilities are stated about things that might happen or, more broadly, about things that might be true. For example, consider the statement 'the probability that Happy Boy wins the 3.15 p.m. race at Kempton Park is 0.12.' The thing that might happen is Happy Boy winning. The statement that might be true is that 'Happy Boy will win'.

It is also generally agreed that **probabilities** are numbers between 0 and 1 inclusive and that a probability of 0 means something is considered certainly not true or not going to happen, while a probability of 1 means it certainly is true or certainly will happen.

Sometimes **probabilities** are expressed as percentages between 0 and 100%. Sometimes they are given as odds, as in '3:1 against', which translates to a probability of 0.25, or 25% if you prefer. Sometimes they are given as proportions as in 'one in four', which is also a probability of 0.25.

Take care when translating between different styles. In the song 'Five to One' by the Doors, Jim Morrison equates 'five to one' with 'one in five', but of course that should be one in six.

2   PROBABILISTIC FORECASTER

It is also clear that **probabilities** come from many sources, which I'll call **probabilistic forecasters**. Mostly they come from people (e.g. weather forecasters, tipsters, research companies, managers in companies), from mathematical formulae, and from computer systems. Some of these **probabilistic forecasters** restrict themselves to a very narrow topic, while others are prepared to give **probabilities** for a wider range of propositions or outcomes.

One question of great interest to auditors and many others is how good the **probabilities** from a particular **probabilistic forecaster** are.

3   CALIBRATION (ALSO KNOWN AS RELIABILITY)

How can you assess the **probabilities** provided by a **probabilistic forecaster**? There are two ways:

1   Look at how the **probabilities** are worked out (which includes looking at any data used).
2   Compare the **probabilities** to reality and see how well they match up.

The second method is the easiest to understand and is easy to do if you have enough data. You can't make any assessment from just one example unless the **probabilistic forecaster** says something is certain and turns out to be wrong.

However, if you have lots of **probabilities** from the same source and you know what actually happened or what the truth was then you can calculate various scores that show how good the source is.

There are two main qualities that good **probabilities** must possess, and one of them is **calibration**.

If a **probabilistic forecaster** of some kind is well **calibrated** then, over time, the frequencies of actual results will agree with the **probabilities** given. For example, suppose for a year a forecaster gives a **probability** of rain tomorrow and we record whether or not there was rain. The forecaster is perfectly **calibrated** if it rained on 10% of the days when the forecaster gave a **probability** of 0.1 of rain, rained on 20% of the days when the forecaster said the **probability** of rain was 0.2, and so on. The extent to which the proportions of days with rain agree with the **probabilities** given for those days is **calibration**.

There are a number of formulae for calculating overall **calibration** across a range of forecasts, but it is a good idea to look at **calibration** at each level of **probability**. A good *average* **calibration** score may hide problems, most likely with poor **calibration** for extreme events.

4   RESOLUTION

Furthermore, **calibration** is not a complete measure of good **probabilities**.

Imagine that, over a typical year, it rains on half the days over a particular town. Every day the forecaster says the **probability** of rain is 0.5, regardless of the season or recent weather, thus demonstrating high **calibration**. We expect more don't we?

The extra thing we expect is that the forecast is responsive to conditions and when the opportunity arises to give **probabilities** for rain that are higher or lower than average the forecaster does so, and in the right direction. These more informative **probabilities** are said to have higher **resolution**. Again, there are alternative formulae for calculating **resolution**.

Higher **resolution** is usually achieved by taking more circumstances into consideration. The weather forecaster could consider not only the identity of the town, but also the season and recent weather. If the forecaster is clever enough to reach the limit of what can be predicted from these circumstances it might be time to gather additional data, perhaps from rainfall radar, weather stations out to sea, and from satellites.

However, there is a limit to how far this can be taken. The more circumstances the forecaster chooses to use, the harder it is to adjust for them all accurately because there are fewer directly comparable past experiences to use as a guide.

A key point to understand is that there is no such thing as *the* **probability** of something happening or being true. We must always think about the **probability** given what knowledge of circumstances we choose to take into consideration, and there are always options to choose from.

The perfect **probabilistic forecaster** would give **probabilities** of rain of 1 or 0, and would always be right. These **probabilities** would have maximum possible **resolution** and **calibration**.

Incidentally, published examples illustrating **calibration** and **resolution** are nearly always in terms of weather forecasting because that is the field of study where these ideas have been developed, but they apply to any **probabilities**.

there is no such thing as **the** probability *of something happening or being true*

5 PROPER SCORE FUNCTION

If you want to motivate a forecaster to give you well **calibrated**, high **resolution probabilities** and want to give some kind of bonus as encouragement then you need to use a **proper score function**.

This is a formula that calculates an overall measure of forecasting skill that gives the forecaster no incentive to lie and every incentive to give the best **probabilities** possible. The Brier Score and the Ignorance function (a logarithmic score) are both **proper score functions**.

Ignorance is a function based in information theory and shows the amount of information, in bits, that learning the outcome provides. For example, if you are certain that an outcome will happen and it does then you receive no information, i.e. you learn nothing you don't already know. However, if your **probability** for that outcome is less than 1 then you will learn something from seeing it happen. If you are convinced that something is impossible and yet it happens then your Ignorance is infinite, an interesting comment on closed mindedness.

probabilities are ... particularly good for thinking about what policies we should adopt

Ignorance can also be interpreted as the time to double your money by betting on outcomes where all outcomes carry equal payouts. Even more interesting is that if you are betting against someone else then your Ignorance needs to be lower than theirs to expect to gain money! Clearly, the quality of **probabilities** has practical importance.

As I mentioned, any approach to assessing **probabilities** needs lots of examples of **probabilities** to work with. Even an idiot can guess right occasionally, so **probabilistic forecasters** need to be judged over a longer term. I often think that **probabilities** are more helpful as a guide to what we should expect over a long series of outcomes, so they are particularly good for thinking about what policies we should adopt.

Probability assessments also need to be made across a defined set of forecasting tasks. For example, it would be grossly unfair to assess a weather forecaster's **calibration** using **probability** judgements for the outcomes of financial investments.

6 AUDIT POINT: JUDGING PROBABILITIES

When people get to practice giving **probabilities** and receive feedback they usually get better at it.

The ideas of **calibration** and **resolution** show that we can judge a person's ability to provide **probabilities**, even if they are just based on gut feelings.

However, to do this we need a reasonable amount of data about **probabilities** they have given and what actually happened. It is also inappropriate for forecasts about things that people will try to change in response to the forecasts.

Some organizations would find that they do have these data and could work out **calibration** and **resolution** numbers, as well as plot graphs showing how **probabilities** given compared to reality.

If that's possible and it hasn't been done, shouldn't it be considered? **Probabilities** might turn out to be surprisingly well **calibrated,** perhaps even to the extent that people feel they can be used in cost-justifying investments in controls. Alternatively, it may be that feedback would be useful for improving the quality of **probabilities** people work with.

7 PROBABILITY INTERPRETATIONS

Not everyone who uses **probabilities** interprets them in the same way and misunderstandings can occur with practical and painful consequences.

The explanations below focus on what most people actually think and do today, rather than going through all the many proposals made by philosophers, scientists, lawyers, and others down the centuries.

Unless you've studied the meaning of **probabilities** in great depth do not assume you know this already!

misunderstandings can occur with practical and painful consequences

8   DEGREE OF BELIEF

In everyday conversations we often say 'probably'. For example, last weekend I was introduced to a man at a party whose name was 'Charles', though I'm not entirely sure now, it was *probably* 'Charles'.

This is **probability** interpreted as a **degree of belief**. Specifically, it is a measure of how much I believe a statement to be true. In my example, the statement was 'The name of the guy was Charles.'

If I think this statement is certainly true then my **probability** of it being true is 1. If I think this is certainly not true then my **probability** of it being true is 0. If I'm not sure either way then my **probability** will be somewhere between these extremes.

This interpretation of **probability** makes it something personal. To Charles (or whoever it was) the name is quite certain. Indeed I was quite a bit more confident when we were first introduced. **Probability** interpreted this way depends on information (and memory!).

However, that doesn't mean it is purely subjective, because these **probability** numbers can still be tested and different people with the same information and instructions should come up with similar numbers.

Interpreting **probabilities** as **degrees of belief** is much more common, more important, and more scientifically respectable than many people think.

In 1946, physicist, mathematician, and electric eel expert Richard Threlkeld Cox (1898–1991) showed how some very simple, common-sense requirements for logical reasoning about uncertain statements led to the laws of mathematical **probability**. He improved on his thinking in 1961 and others have also refined it, notably Edwin Thompson Jaynes (1922–1998), another physicist, writing shortly before his death.

When stating **probabilities** it is good practice to make clear what information about the circumstances of your prediction you are using. As mentioned earlier, different choices will give different **probabilities**.

For example, if you are referring to your **degree of belief** that it will rain on your garden tomorrow you might decide to take into account nothing about the seasons or the weather, or you could say 'given that it is a day in August', or 'given that the weather forecast on TV said it would rain all day', and so on.

You can't say 'given all the facts' because tomorrow's weather would be one of them, and saying 'given all the facts I know now' is likely to lead to confusion as your knowledge continues to increase over time. Ideally you should make a clear, sensible choice, and communicate it.

9 SITUATION (ALSO KNOWN AS AN EXPERIMENT)

Other common interpretations of **probability** focus on the narrower topic of outcomes. This is the explanation most likely to be shown in a textbook on **probability**.

The outcomes in question are those of a **situation,** or **experiment** (e.g. tossing a coin, drawing a card from a shuffled deck, driving a car for a year and recording the cost of damage to it, paying the total claims on an insurance policy).

The word **experiment** is rather misleading because it doesn't have to be an experiment in the usual sense. It is really just any situation where the outcome has yet to be discovered by the person who is doing the thinking. This includes things that have yet to happen and also things that have happened but whose outcome is not yet known to the thinker.

In this book I've used the word **situation** instead of **experiment** to help you keep an open mind.

Situations are things we have to define, and to some extent they are an arbitrary choice. They define a collection of, perhaps many, episodes in real life that have happened and/or may happen in the future. Each of these episodes will be unique in some way, but if they meet our

clear definition is important

definition of the **situation** then they are examples of it. For example, 'drawing a card from a shuffled deck' could be our choice of **situation**, but it might have been 'drawing a card from a shuffled deck of Happy Families cards' or 'drawing the top card from a deck of ordinary playing cards shuffled by a professional conjuror.'

In effect our choice of **situation** is the same as our choice of which circumstances to take into consideration.

Our choice of **situation** makes a difference, and clear definition is important.

10   LONG RUN RELATIVE FREQUENCY

Another common interpretation of **probabilities** focuses on the outcomes from **situations** we see as inherently difficult or even impossible to predict.

Suppose I vigorously flip a fair coin in the traditional way. What is the **probability** of getting heads? Most people will answer confidently that it is 50% or ½ or 0.5, or perhaps 50:50, or evens, depending on their preferred language. This is a **probability** we feel we know.

An idea that captures a lot of our intuitions about **probability** is that it has something to do with what would happen if we could study the outcomes of many examples of a **situation**.

If we could toss that fair coin billions of times and record the proportion of heads we would expect it to be very close to 50% (see Figure 1). So, when we say the **probability** of heads next time is 0.5 that is consistent with the idea that if we did the same thing lots of times then half the time the outcome would be heads.

In this interpretation, **probability** is a property of the real world independent of our knowledge of it.

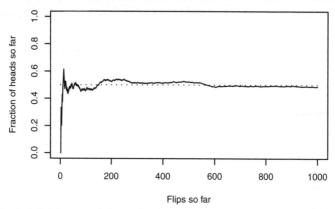

Figure 1 Gradually converging on the long run relative frequency of heads from flipping a fair coin

For this book I've called this the **long run relative frequency (LRRF)**.

As ever, our choice of which **situation** we imagine repeating is crucial and any given occasion could be an example of many different **situations**.

Probability numbers, as always, must lie between zero and one. Zero means that heads never turns up, while one means it always does.

11 DEGREE OF BELIEF ABOUT LONG RUN RELATIVE FREQUENCY

Unfortunately, **probability** based purely on **long run relative frequency** doesn't always score well on Ignorance and other forecasting skill scores. The problem is that it ignores an additional source of uncertainty that is often present.

Imagine I vigorously flip a coin that is clearly bent. What would you say is the **probability** of getting heads this time?

It feels different doesn't it? Our basic schooling on **probability** tends to focus on **situations** like card games, dice rolling, and coin tossing where we usually assume we know what the **long run relative frequencies** should be because we assume that all outcomes are equally likely. Problems set in school textbooks usually say that the coin is 'fair', meaning that you can assume the usual **probabilities**.

In real life things are rarely so convenient. Individual outcomes aren't always equally likely. We don't know exactly what the **long run relative frequencies** would be. We're uncertain about them. Coins look a bit bent and are tossed by conjurors we don't trust. We can't repeat things billions of times. We have to make estimates.

So, here's another interpretation. **Probability** can also mean our **degree of belief** about **long run relative frequencies**.

In this interpretation **probability** depends on our knowledge. The real world has a **long run relative frequency** and statements about that are what the **degrees of belief** apply to.

We can't repeat things billions of times. We have to make estimates

Mathematicians sometimes use **probability** to mean just **long run relative frequency**. On other occasions they use **probability** to mean their **degree of belief about long run relative frequency**. They may even use both ideas in the same problem, calling them both **probability**. Using the same name both times is confusing so separating the two ideas can be very helpful.

12 DEGREE OF BELIEF ABOUT AN OUTCOME

Mathematicians sometimes use **probability** to mean **degree of belief about an outcome**. For example, the statement 'heads next time' could be true or false. This interpretation of **probability** applies the **degree of belief** idea to a statement like that.

The **degree of belief** about an outcome can be calculated from the **long run relative frequency** and the **degree of belief about long run relative frequency**. Alternatively, you can just jump to a **degree of belief about an outcome** by some other means, such as intuition.

I know the different **probability interpretations** take a while to sink in but stick at it because this is where some huge practical mistakes have been made. Here's an example that might just do it for you.

Picture that bent coin I flipped a page ago and imagine you had the opportunity to flip it and learn more about its tendency to come up heads. From a handful of flips you couldn't know the true **long run relative frequency** of that coin. That means you don't know the **probability** of heads in the **long run relative frequency** sense.

However, you could start to form a view about what are more likely values for the **probability** (**LRRF** interpretation) and you could express this in terms of **probabilities** (**degree of belief about LRRF** interpretation) that each **LRRF** is the true one.

So what is the **probability** of getting heads next time that you would use for gambling purposes? (This is the one that represents your **degree of belief** that the outcome will be 'heads' and is your **probability** in the **degree of belief about an outcome** interpretation.)

That **probability** you could get by intuition (the traditional way) or by combining the **probability** (**LRRF** interpretation) with the other **probabilities** (**degree of belief about LRRF** interpretation) in a particular way to get to a **probability** (**degree of belief about an outcome** interpretation).

The theory of **probability** works fine whichever interpretation you use, but the problems come when different interpretations get confused or inappropriately left out.

13   AUDIT POINT: MISMATCHED INTERPRETATIONS OF PROBABILITY

Obviously things can go wrong if one person means **probability** in one sense and another thinks they mean something else. We can even confuse ourselves.

Ask someone for the **probability** of heads from tossing an unfamiliar bent coin and many will answer 'I don't know', revealing that they are thinking in **long run relative frequency** terms. They are seeing **probabilities** as characteristics of the real world, independent of their knowledge of them.

Take that same person to their favourite sporting event and ask them what they think of the odds on a famous competitor and they will happily take a view. This is true even though they still don't know what the **long run relative frequency** of that competitor winning that event is, and could never know it. In this context they activate the **degree of belief about an outcome** interpretation, without realizing they have done so.

The most dangerous version of this confusion is where one person is thinking in terms of **long run relative frequencies** and offers **probability** information to someone else who thinks they are getting **degree of belief about an outcome** information.

The speaker is giving what could be wild guesses about the real world, without mentioning that they are guesses. The listener does not realize this crucial information is being left out. In this simple misunderstanding uncertainty is ignored and the listener comes away thinking things are much better understood than they really are. This happens so often that I will be returning to it repeatedly in this book.

14 AUDIT POINT: IGNORING UNCERTAINTY ABOUT PROBABILITIES

Focusing on **long run relative frequencies** and forgetting that we aren't certain of them is a mistake. It may happen due to mismatched interpretations of **probability**, or it may be that the uncertainty is ignored for some other reason, such as convenience or a desire to seem authoritative.

Whatever the reason, the consequence is that risks are generally underestimated and too little is done to use available data to help get a better view.

15 AUDIT POINT: NOT USING DATA TO ILLUMINATE PROBABILITIES

People often fail to use available data to firm up **probabilities**. This may be because they think of **probabilities** as nothing more than subjective guesses about outcomes.

More often it is because they focus on the **long run relative frequency** idea and think any data used must be from past occurrences of the *identical* circumstances to those now expected. Unable to find data that are from identical circumstances in the past, they give up on data altogether.

Identical circumstances never happen; that would require repeating the history of the universe. What does happen is recurrence of circumstances that match the definition of one or more **situations** that we have chosen. It is also possible to generate quite good **probabilities** by taking into account the degree of similarity between **situations**.

The trick is to think of definitions for **situations** that include the occasion for which we want a **probability**, seem to capture a lot of what is important, and for which we have data.

In doing so we must accept that the more narrowly we define the **situation**, the more relevant past data will be, but the fewer data we will have to work with. Put another way, narrow **situation** definitions give us high uncertainty about highly informative **long run relative frequencies**.

For example, a construction company that builds houses, flats, and some large buildings like schools might have years of data on estimated and actual costs and times to complete its projects. It would be a mistake to think that, because every project is unique in some way, past experience is no guide to future cost estimates. It might be that using data from its house construction in the last two years gives a helpful distribution of estimates that, at the very least, enables baseless optimism to be challenged.

The key points are that we don't need to repeat identical circumstances and may have more relevant data than we realize.

16 OUTCOME SPACE (ALSO KNOWN AS SAMPLE SPACE, OR POSSIBILITY SPACE)

Having covered the main **interpretations** of **probability** it's time to go back to the idea of a **situation** and explain some more of the thinking and terminology behind the most common textbook version of **probability** theory.

In this approach, the next thing to define for a **situation** is its **outcome space**, otherwise known as its **sample space** or **possibility space**. This is the set of all possible elementary outcomes from the **situation**. We also need a way to name or otherwise refer to the outcomes.

For example, tossing a coin once is usually said to have the **outcome space** {heads, tails} but if you let it drop onto a muddy sports field it might be more accurate to say {heads, tails, edge}. If you prefer shorter names then that could instead be {h, t, e}. It's another option.

What is an elementary outcome? That's something else to be decided and written down. There are options and to some extent the decision is an arbitrary one. However, some choices are easier to work with than others. For example, if you can define your outcomes in such a way that they are equally likely, then that makes life a lot easier.

Sometimes the outcomes are more like combinations of outcomes. For example, the outcomes from tossing two coins one after the other could be defined as {(H,H), (H,T), (T,H), (T,T)} with the first letter representing one coin and the second representing the other. Another example would be measurements of newborn babies, where each outcome could be represented by a bundle of facts such as its weight, length, sex, and skin colour.

In real life **situations** we usually have a number of different ways to characterize what could happen. For example, we might be interested in health and safety, or money, or time. Each possibility, if chosen, will give us a different **outcome space**.

The phrase **sample space** is what the mathematicians most often use, for historical reasons, but it is misleading (again) because sampling in the usual sense isn't normally involved. In this book I've used the less common term **outcome space** so you don't have to keep reminding yourself to forget about sampling.

---

17   AUDIT POINT: UNSPECIFIED SITUATIONS

Many so-called 'risks' for which people are asked to give a 'probability' do not describe adequately the **situation** they apply to. For example, there may be a 'risk of theft' but over what time period, involving which assets, and measured in what way? Unless this vagueness is cleared up it's hard to say anything meaningful about how big the 'risk' is, even broadly and without numbers.

Consider reviewing a sample of risk descriptions and recommending some kind of quality improvement work.

Different styles of risk analysis require clarity on different points, so you are looking for any statement that seems vague and should also consider whether important qualifications have been left out altogether. It is very common to forget to state the time period for a 'risk'. For example, 'Risk of theft in the next year' is much less likely than 'Risk of theft at any time in the future.'

18   OUTCOMES REPRESENTED WITHOUT NUMBERS

The outcomes in an **outcome space** can be represented in a variety of ways. One way is without numbers. For example, if beads of different colours are put into a bag and shaken, and then one is drawn out, the outcomes might be represented by colours, e.g. {Red, Blue, Green }.

This is important because some concepts in risk mathematics do not apply if the outcomes are not represented by numbers.

A lot of the things we call risks and put on risk registers are worded so that there are just two outcomes and they're not represented by numbers. Those two outcomes are {'The risk happens', 'The risk does not happen'}.

if the risk is 'Loss of market share' then surely it matters how much market share is lost

This is simple, but usually much *too* simple and tends to mean we cannot think about important nuances. For example, if the risk is 'Loss of market share' then surely it matters how much market share is lost. The problem is not lack of numbers but failure to capture the richness of potential outcomes. Most mathematical risk analysis is much more informative.

19 OUTCOMES REPRESENTED WITH NUMBERS

In other **outcome spaces** the outcomes are represented by numbers.

20 RANDOM VARIABLE

Often what people are interested in is not the outcome but, instead, a number that depends on the outcome. For example, if you roll two dice when playing Monopoly it is the total of the dice you care about.

And when people enter a lottery they are interested in how many of the balls selected at random in the draw match the balls they bet on. They are not really interested in exactly which balls are drawn. A lot of risk management in businesses focuses on money.

A **random variable** is, strictly speaking, neither random nor a variable, but is a rule that links each outcome to a unique number. Given an outcome it returns the appropriate number. People often talk about **random variables** as if they represent the actual outcome (which is not yet known). In other words, they treat them as if they are the numbers returned rather than the rule, but this usually doesn't lead to mistakes.

Random variables, by convention, always return what mathematicians call 'real' numbers, which for our purposes just means they don't have to be whole numbers, but can be anywhere on the continuous number line.

Sometimes the way outcomes are linked to numbers can seem a bit arbitrary. For example, when the outcome space is {success, failure} these outcomes are often mapped to one and zero respectively.

Traditionally, **random variables** are usually given names that are capital letters from the English alphabet and the runaway favourite choices are X and Y.

In practice the definition of a **random variable** is a matter of choice and needs to be clear.

21 EVENT

An **event**, in mathematics, means a subset of the **outcome space**. For example, if you've chosen the **situation** of tossing a coin and letting it fall on a muddy sports field and the **outcome space** {heads, tails, edge} then you could define a number of possible **events** having one or more outcomes in them, such as an **event** you could call 'valid outcome' defined as the set {heads, tails}.

What **events** are defined is yet another free choice. The **event** 'valid outcome' is likely to be useful when talking about coin tossing on a muddy field, but of course you could look at it in other ways.

Events involving discrete outcomes can be defined by listing all the outcomes included or by stating some rule for membership.

Events involving outcomes that could be anywhere on a continuum of numbers are often defined by giving the top and bottom of the range of numbers to be included in the event. Another common technique is to give one number, defining the **event** as all outcomes with numbers less than or equal to that number.

Random variables can be used to succinctly define **events**. For example, if the name X is given to a **random variable** returning the total of two fair dice thrown together then:

1 $\{X = 4\}$ is the event that contains all the outcomes that add up to 4, i.e. $\{(1,3), (2,2), (3,1)\}$; and
2 $\{X < 3\}$ is the event that contains all the outcomes that add up to less than 3, i.e. $\{(1,1)\}$.

This is the traditional notation and I hope it is clear what is intended. If not then it may be that you've noticed the mistake, which is to write as if X is the value returned by the **random variable**, not the **random variable** itself. Perhaps a clearer notation would be something like

$\{X(w) = 4\}$ where w represents the outcome from the **situation**, and $X(w)$ is the usual way to show the value returned when a function (e.g. X) is applied to an input value (e.g. w).

An **event** is not necessarily something sudden, dramatic, or memorable. This idea is very different to our ordinary idea of an 'event' and this causes some confusion. Procedures for risk management tend to be written as if 'events' are dramatic things with all or nothing results, like explosions. But in reality most situations where 'risk' needs to be managed are not like this. There are a few explosions but far more slightly surprising outcomes of undramatic **situations**. It is better to use the mathematical idea of an **event** and this is more consistent with the vast majority of 'risks' that people think of.

An event is not necessarily something sudden, dramatic, or memorable

22 AUDIT POINT: EVENTS WITH UNSPECIFIED BOUNDARIES

Many 'risks' on risk registers have a form like 'inadequate human resources'. We imagine a scale of human resources and a zone towards the bottom that is 'inadequate'. Unfortunately, the level below which human resources are inadequate is unspecified (and probably unknown) making the 'risk' unspecified too.

23   AUDIT POINT: MISSING RANGES

Another problem with 'risks' like 'inadequate human resources' is that the choice of the word 'inadequate' is rarely the result of careful thought. It could have been replaced by 'less than expected' or 'zero' with little comment by most people. Choosing 'inadequate' as the definition for the **event** removes from consideration other ranges that might be surprising and require planning for. I call these *missing ranges*. They are very easy to check for and point out.

24   AUDIT POINT: TOP 10 RISK REPORTING

Many people in senior positions have been encouraged to believe that they need to focus on the 'top 10 risks'. I wonder how they would feel if they understood that **events** are defined by people and can be redefined to suit their purposes.

Imagine you are a manager in a risk workshop and somebody has just suggested a risk for inclusion in a risk register that (1) you would obviously be responsible for, (2) will probably be in the top 10, and (3) you can't do much about. You don't want the risk to be in the top 10 and to get beaten up by the Board every quarter so you say, 'That's a really interesting risk, but I think to understand it fully we need to analyse it into its key elements.'

You then start to hack the big 'risk' into smaller 'risks', keeping on until every component is small enough to stay out of the top 10.

The point is that the size of a 'risk' is heavily influenced by how widely it is defined. Most of the time the level of aggregation of risks is something we set without much thought, so whether something gets into the top 10 or not is partly luck.

Auditors should highlight this issue when found and suggest either the level of aggregation of 'risks' be controlled in some way or top 10 reporting be abandoned and replaced by a better way of focusing attention.

25 PROBABILITY OF AN OUTCOME

In researching for this book I consulted several different sources and got several different explanations of **probability** theory, with slightly different terminology and slightly different notation.

The reason for this is historical and understanding it may help to make sense of it all.

In the beginning, **probability** theory was focused on winning in games of chance. It concentrated on situations where there was just a finite number of outcomes, such as the roll of a die, or a hand in a card game.

It made perfect sense to talk about the **probability of an outcome** and to calculate the **probability** of an **event** by adding up the **probabilities** of the outcomes they included. (Remember that an **event** is a subset of the **outcome space**, so it's a set of outcomes.)

The sum of the **probabilities** of all the outcomes from a **situation** is one, because it is certain that one of those outcomes will result, by definition.

Later, people moved on to think about **situations** where the outcomes could be any point on a continuum, such as the life of an electric light bulb. In this example the life could be, theoretically, any amount of time. Even between a lifetime of 10 minutes and a lifetime of 11 minutes there is an infinite number of possible lifetimes. (In practice we can't measure accurately enough to recognize that many but in principle it is true.)

This revealed an awkward problem. The **probability of the outcome** being *exactly* equal to any particular point on the continuum seemed to drop to zero, and yet the outcome had to be somewhere on the continuum. How can adding up lots of zeroes give the result one?

To get around this problem, **probability** was defined in a different way specifically for these continuum situations, but still starting with outcomes and building up from there.

26   PROBABILITY OF AN EVENT

Then in 1933 the Russian mathematician Andrey Nikolaevich Kolmogorov (1903–1987) did some very fancy maths and showed how both problems (with and without outcomes on a continuum) could be dealt with using one approach.

Although Kolmogorov's approach has been accepted for decades it still hasn't reached every textbook and website.

Kolmogorov's thinking is a mass of mind-boggling terminology and notation (which I'm not going to go into) and was mostly concerned with applying the fashionable ideas of measure theory to **probability**. Yet one of the key ideas behind it is simple: since starting with **probabilities for outcomes** hasn't worked neatly for us, let's start with **probabilities for events** instead.

27   PROBABILITY MEASURE (ALSO KNOWN AS PROBABILITY DISTRIBUTION, PROBABILITY FUNCTION, OR EVEN PROBABILITY DISTRIBUTION FUNCTION)

The result of Kolmogorov's hard work was the notion of a magical thing called a **probability measure** that tells you what **probability** number is associated with each **event**. (The word 'measure' here indicates Kolmogorov was using measure theory, but you don't have to in order to associate **probability** numbers with **events**.)

The alternative name **probability function** (which lacks the link to measure theory) is a good one because, in mathematics, a function is simply a rule, table, or formula that takes one or more inputs and consistently replies with a particular output. For example, a function called something like 'square' might return the square of each number given to it. (A **random variable** is also a function.)

In the case of **probability**, you tell the **probability function** which **event** you are interested in and it returns the **probability** that goes with it.

The alternative names are used in different ways by different authors, which can be confusing, particularly when **probability distribution** is used to refer to something that does not give **probabilities**.

The way the **probability measure** is designed depends on what type of outcome is involved and what is a convenient way to identify the **event**.

For example, if the **outcome space** for coloured balls pulled out of a bag is {Red, Blue, White, Black} then a **probability function** called Pr (one of the common name choices) might be used, as in these examples:

1 Pr({White}) = 0.3 means that the **probability** of pulling out a white ball is 0.3.
2 Pr({Black}) = 0.2, means that the **probability** of pulling out a black ball is 0.2.
3 Pr(Monochrome) = 0.5, where Monochrome = {White, Black}, means that the **probability** of pulling out a black or white ball is 0.5.

In writing these examples for you I've been quite strict and made sure that the thing inside the ( ) parentheses is a set of outcomes. However, the notation used is not always so careful.

Remember that **events** can also be specified using **random variables**.

The impact of Kolmogorov's work may have been huge for the theoretical foundations of **probability**, but it has made little impact otherwise so most of us don't need to know any more about it.

28   CONDITIONAL PROBABILITIES

Mathematicians have a habit of leaving out information to keep their formulae looking simple, expecting readers to guess the rest from the context.

Formulae about **probabilities** give countless examples of this. The usual way to write 'the **probability** of event A occurring' is:

$P(A)$

Mathematicians have a habit of leaving out information to keep their formulae looking simple

But what **situation** are we talking about? What is the **outcome space**? Or, put it another way, what parts of our knowledge about the circumstances surrounding the **event** of interest are we choosing to use for the purposes of this **probability** number? For example, if we are interested in the outcome of tossing a coin, do we say this is an example of coin tossing, of tossing this particular coin, or of coin tossing on a muddy field? If the coin is to be flipped by a conjuror do we take into account the fact that he has just bet us £100 it will be heads?

Usually, little or even none of this is stated in the formula, with the obvious risk of confusion or mistakes. For good reason, people sometimes point out that *all* **probabilities** are **conditional probabilities**.

However, there is a standard notation for showing information that defines the **situation** or otherwise shows what parts of our knowledge of circumstances are being used. This is the notation for **conditional probabilities**. For example, a way to write 'the **probability** of event A occurring given this is an instance of a **situation** with outcome space S' is this:

$P(A \mid S)$

You say this to yourself as 'the **probability** of *A* given *S*.'

When new information arrives we are not obliged to use it in every **probability** we state. However, for **probabilities** where we do use the new information this effectively redefines the **situation**.

For example, suppose our initial **situation** was 'drawing a playing card from a shuffled deck' but later we learn that the deck has been shuffled and the card drawn by a conjuror. This new information redefines the **situation** quite dramatically.

In symbols, if we want to show 'the **probability** of event *A* occurring given this is an instance of a **situation** with outcome space *S*, and given the outcome is already known to be within event *B*', we write:

$$P(A \mid S, B)$$

In this particular example this makes the new outcome space, in effect, *B*, because *B* is entirely within *S*.

For some, perhaps all, occasions where we want to use **probabilities** the addition of more and more information might eventually allow us to predict the outcome with complete certainty, in theory.

29 DISCRETE RANDOM VARIABLES

At this point **probability** theory starts to focus on **events** defined using **random variables**.

Random variables are functions that give 'real' values, i.e. numbers that could, in principle, lie anywhere on a continuous number line from zero all the way up to infinity (∞), and indeed from zero all the way down through minus numbers to minus infinity ($-\infty$). In symbols, they are in the range ($-\infty, \infty$).

However, when a **random variable** is defined for the **outcome space** of a **situation**, it may well be limited to returning just certain values within that huge range. For example, if the **random variable** represents the total of two dice then it can only take the specific values 2, 3, 4, 5, 6, 7, 8, 9, 10, 11, or 12, even though it is a real number.

Random variables are classified into three types according to the values they can return once hooked up to an **outcome space**. The simplest type is the **discrete random variable**.

Discrete random variables can return only a finite number of values, or an infinite but countable number of values.

To illustrate the meaning of 'countable', the set of numbers {1, 2, 3 … and so on forever} has infinitely many elements but they are countable, whereas the number of numbers on the real number line between 0 and 1 is infinite and not countable. Countable infinity is much smaller!

30 CONTINUOUS RANDOM VARIABLES

The other type of **random variable** that gets a lot of attention is the **continuous random variable**. This type (1) can return an uncountably infinite number of values but (2) the **probability** of returning any particular value is always zero.

That usually means that the value is somewhere on a continuum of numbers and no particular value is special.

If your brain is still functioning at this point you may be wondering how the **probability** can always be zero. Surely an outcome of some kind is inevitable, by definition, so the sum of the **probabilities** for all the individual outcomes must be one. How can the sum of lots of zeros be anything other than zero?

Good question, and perhaps it makes more sense to think of those zeroes actually being infinitesimally small 'nearly zeroes' so that what is really happening is that infinitely many infinitesimally small things are being added together. Only by cunning mathematical reasoning can the value of such a sum be worked out.

A huge proportion of the applied risk analysis done by mathematicians in business and elsewhere involves **continuous random variables** (though it is not necessary to go through the reasoning about infinity each time).

Incidentally, the Ignorance function mentioned in connection with **proper scoring rules** can only be applied to **discrete random variables**, but applying it to **continuous random variables** simply involves slicing the continuous case into lots of little pieces. This is just a reminder that in most cases where we **model** the world with continuous variables the reality is that we cannot and do not measure to infinite accuracy. Money, for example, is usually tracked to two decimal places, not to infinite precision, which would involve quoting some numbers to infinitely many decimal places!

the reality is that we cannot and do not measure to infinite accuracy

31 MIXED RANDOM VARIABLES (ALSO KNOWN AS MIXED DISCRETE-CONTINUOUS RANDOM VARIABLES)

Discrete and **continuous random variables** get so much attention it is easy to get the impression that they are the only types that exist. Not so, and in fact **random variables** of the third type are applicable to most of the 'risks' people put on risk registers.

These forgotten **random variables** are so unloved that it took me a while to find their proper name: **mixed random variables**.

Like the **continuous random variables** they can take an uncountably infinite number of values, but these hybrids can give special values whose **probability** of occurrence is more than zero.

For example, suppose that the **random variable** is for the useful life of a light bulb. Some light bulbs don't work at all, while others go on for a period we don't know in advance.

This means that the **probability** of lasting exactly zero seconds is more than zero, but the **probability** of any particular lifespan beyond this is zero.

---

32 AUDIT POINT: IGNORING MIXED RANDOM VARIABLES

Perhaps because they don't get much attention **mixed random variables** tend to get left out.

People don't think of using them in their risk analysis and instead behave as if everything is either discrete or continuous.

This is important because such a high proportion of 'risks' on risk registers are best described by a **mixed random variable**.

It is true that there are very few well known distribution types that are mixed and software does not support them directly, in most cases. However, a mixed type can easily be built from a combination of **discrete** and **continuous random variables**.

For example, to express the lifespan of a light bulb you can use a **discrete random variable** to say if it fails immediately or not, and then a **continuous random variable** to show the **probability distribution** of its lifespan assuming it at least gets started.

Be alert for this mistake when reviewing risk management procedures, templates, and models.

33 CUMULATIVE PROBABILITY DISTRIBUTION FUNCTION

There is one type of **probability distribution function** that can capture, and graph, the nuances of **random variables** of any type.

This kind of function is called a **cumulative probability distribution function**. It gives the **probability** that the value returned by a **random variable** will be *less than or equal to* any particular value.

The graph of a **cumulative probability distribution function** always rises from left to right, as in Figure 2.

Take a moment to think this through a few times because we are not used to seeing this kind of graph.

Cumulative probability distribution functions are extremely useful in risk analysis because they can be used in many different situations, even when other types of function are too fussy to be applied.

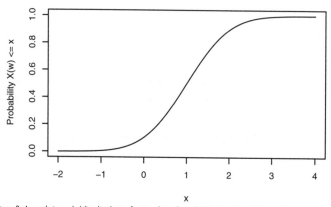

Figure 2 A cumulative probability distribution function shows the probability that the random variable returns a value less than or equal to x

For example, suppose a 'risk' has been written that says 'The cost of fire damage to our warehouses during this year.' Imagine that there's a good chance that this will be zero, because fires are rare. However, if a fire starts then the cost could be anywhere from tiny (a slight scorching) to catastrophic, with a large building burned to the ground.

A **cumulative probability distribution function** can capture all this. For cost values less than zero (we gain money) the cumulative **probability** is zero. That's not going to happen. At a cost of exactly zero the **probability** will be the chance of no fire damage during the year. For higher and higher values of cost the cumulative **probability** will gradually increase, ultimately getting closer and closer to one (see Figure 3).

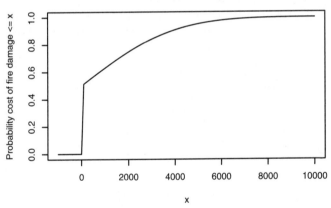

Figure 3 Cumulative probability distribution function for cost of fire damage, x

34 AUDIT POINT: IGNORING IMPACT SPREAD

The usual treatment of items on a risk register is to ask people for the probability of 'it' happening and the impact if 'it' does.

But what if the impact could be anything over a wide range? For example, how do you estimate a single impact level for a risk item like 'Loss of market share'? Surely it depends on how much market share is lost, among other things. I call this 'impact spread' and my study of published risk registers shows that virtually all risk register items have impact spread for at least one reason and often for several.

The question on the risk register requires an answer that is a single number or category, and there are several ways people could choose one. They could pick the first level of impact within the range that comes to mind. They could pick the level that seems most representative, or most likely, or is the **probability** weighted average of the whole range, or a halfway point, take something at random, or pick something that combines with the **probability** number to give the priority rating they think the 'risk' should have.

If we want the impact ratings to mean something then we need to define how people should reduce the range to a single point, or change our technique.

The two recommendations auditors should consider first are these:

- Define the required impact rating as the **probability** weighted average impact over the whole range of possibilities. This means that when it is combined with the **probability** it gives something meaningful.
- Change the rating system so that it asks for a **probability** of at least some impact, and then the **probability** of impact greater than one or more other thresholds. This technique elicits a simplified variant of the **cumulative probability distribution function** and is easier to explain.

35 AUDIT POINT: CONFUSING MONEY AND UTILITY

When we talk about 'impact' another possible confusion is between a measure such as money and how much we value the money. The word 'utility' is often used to mean the real value we perceive in something.

For example, a financial loss like losing £1 million is surely more important if this amount would destroy your company.

When we talk casually about 'impact' there is always the danger of overlooking this point and flipping from thinking in money terms to acting as if it is really utility we are talking about.

The two ways of thinking give different answers. Suppose we have two 'risks', one of which can lead to losses in a narrow range, with the average being £100,000. The other also has an average of £100,000 but the range of possibilities is much larger with a possibility of losses that ruin the company.

Is it fair to treat these two losses as having the same impact? In financial terms their average is the same but if we translate to utility and *then* take the average the second risk is considerably worse.

Some organizations try to express a 'risk appetite', which is supposed to help employees respond consistently and appropriately to risks, especially the bigger ones. If averages (or other midpoints) from money impact distributions are being used then the risk appetite initiative is seriously undermined.

36 PROBABILITY MASS FUNCTION

A fussier probability distribution is the **probability mass function**, which only applies to **discrete random variables** (see Figure 4).

A **probability mass function** gives the **probability** that the **random variable** will return any particular value.

The importance of **probability mass functions** perhaps goes back to the early focus on the **probabilities** of outcomes as opposed to **events**.

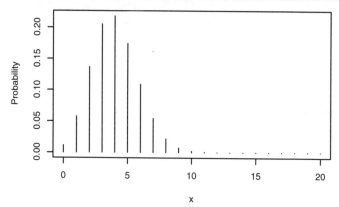

Figure 4 A probability mass function

Also, if you have the **probability mass function** then you can calculate the **probability of any event**.

37 PROBABILITY DENSITY FUNCTION

Obviously a **probability mass function** won't work with a **continuous random variable** because the **probability** of any particular value being returned is always zero, and that's a problem with the **mixed type** too.

For **continuous random variables** only it is possible to create a function called a **probability density function** that returns not **probability**, but something called **probability** *density*.

Graphs like the one in Figure 5 have **probability density** on the vertical axis, not **probability**, so in that sense they are not **probability distributions** at all.

The *area* under one of these **probability density function** graphs is what represents the **probability**. If you want to know the **probability** that the **random variable** will return a value somewhere between two

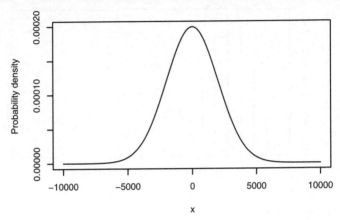

Figure 5 A probability density function

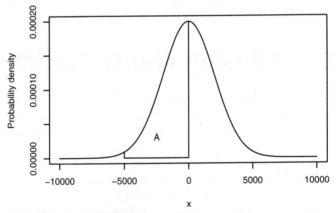

Figure 6 The area, A, under the curve is the probability of x being between −5000 and 0

numbers then you need the area under the **probability density function** curve that lies between those two values. The total area under the curve is always one (see Figure 6).

Again, the importance of **probability density functions** perhaps goes back to the days when **probability** theory was focused on outcomes. They are an attempt to give a number for each possible outcome, which is sort of like **probability** even though it isn't **probability**. If you have the **probability density function** then you can calculate the **probability of any event**.

38   SHARPNESS

One quality of **probabilities** that tends to contribute to high **resolution** is **sharpness**. **Sharpness** is simply use of **probabilities** that are near to zero or one, and it does not imply that those **probabilities** are also well **calibrated**.

The choice of the word **sharpness** is now easy to understand in terms of **probability density functions**.

Imagine Figures 7(a) and 7(b) represent forecasts for the change in value of a portfolio of investments over two periods of 24 hours. In Figure 7(a), which is for the first period of 24 hours, one forecast-

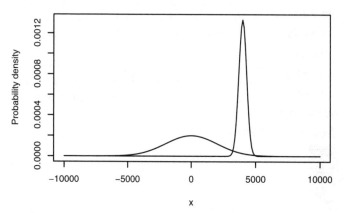

Figure 7 (a) Forecasts for the first day with a wide distribution and a much sharper distribution, equally well calibrated

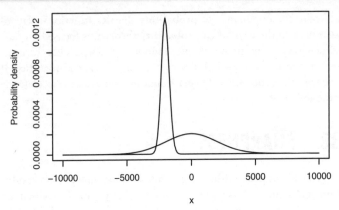

Figure 7 (b) Forecasts for the second day with the wide distribution unchanged but the sharp distribution more responsive to circumstances

The more we try to take into consideration, the less directly relevant past experience we can draw on

ing approach gives a well **calibrated** but widely spread **probability distribution** while the other, equally well **calibrated**, distribution is much **sharper**. Figure 7(b) shows the forecasts for the second period of 24 hours and the widely spread distribution is unchanged while the **sharp** forecast has taken more circumstances into account and is different from the previous day.

The more we try to take into consideration, the less directly relevant past experience we can draw on. We have the chance to achieve high **resolution**, but without much history as a guide we risk poor **calibration**. It's a balancing act and understanding it is a hot research topic.

39   RISK

Finally, we have arrived at **risk**. The reason for your long wait is that mathematicians don't really have much use for the word in either of its main senses.

In everyday conversations we often talk about 'risks', meaning nasty possibilities that can be listed and counted. Mathematicians have **events** and **random variables** instead, and they are much better defined ideas, free from the associations with danger and losses that tend to make 'risk' an entirely negative idea.

In everyday conversations we also talk about how much 'risk' we face, meaning a *quantity* of some nasty possibility. The concept of **probability** was invented centuries ago and when combined with values of outcomes it does everything that 'risk' does and so much more.

*the idea of ...
a number that
represents some
notion of 'risk'
has caught on*

However, there is a mathematically oriented concept of **risk**. Its development may owe something to influential work on portfolio theory by American economist Harry Markowitz (1927–), in which he used a number to represent the spread of possible returns from investments and called it 'risk'. This was done to make some of his mathematics more convenient and is justified only by some rather specific assumptions about how investors value investment returns and about how those returns are distributed. However, these finer points have long been ignored and the idea of applying a formula to a **probability distribution** to produce a number that represents some notion of 'risk' has caught on.

In this approach, **risk** is a number calculated using a function that takes as its input the **probability distribution** of a **random variable**.

There is no agreed function for calculating **risk**. There are already several to choose from and more will probably be invented in future. Under close scrutiny all of these have shortcomings.

Before I explain some of these alternative **risk** functions it will be helpful to explain something that is often used as part of them and is generally very useful.

40   MEAN VALUE OF A PROBABILITY DISTRIBUTION (ALSO KNOWN AS THE EXPECTED VALUE)

Another function that takes a **probability distribution** as input and returns a number is the **mean**, otherwise known by the highly misleading name of **expected value**. This is the **probability** weighted average of all outcomes, and only works when the outcomes are represented as numbers.

For example, if we think of the **probability mass function** for a fair die rolled properly, then the outcomes and their **probabilities** are:

$$P(1) = \frac{1}{6}, P(2) = \frac{1}{6}, P(3) = \frac{1}{6},$$

$$P(4) = \frac{1}{6}, P(5) = \frac{1}{6}, \text{ and } P(6) = \frac{1}{6}$$

The **probability** weighted average of these is:

$$1 \times \frac{1}{6} + 2 \times \frac{1}{6} + 3 \times \frac{1}{6} + 4 \times \frac{1}{6} + 5 \times \frac{1}{6} + 6 \times \frac{1}{6} = 3\frac{1}{2}$$

No, I haven't made a mistake; the **expected value** from rolling a die is 3½ – which is an impossible outcome. In this case the **expected value** is also an impossible value.

In ordinary language, if we 'expect' something that means we either think it jolly well ought to happen or that it is more likely than not. In mathematics, an **expected value** does not need to be more likely than not and might not even be possible.

---

41   AUDIT POINT: EXCESSIVE FOCUS ON EXPECTED VALUES

When **expected values** come into a conversation (e.g. about forecasts) other outcomes tend to be forgotten. An **expected value** supported by pages of spreadsheeting gets a credibility it rarely deserves.

Auditors should check for this in a variety of situations and recommend taking a broader view and considering more possible futures.

---

42   AUDIT POINT: MISUNDERSTANDING 'EXPECTED'

The word 'expected' has two ordinary meanings as well as its mathematical meaning and this can lead to confusion.

First, people might think that 'expected' means 'more likely than not', i.e. a fairly highly level of confidence in a prediction. If the business case for a project says its value is 'expected' to be £2.5 million then non-mathematical readers might think that means a very confident prediction of a value of exactly £2.5 million (give or take a few thousand perhaps). It could really mean that the project's proposers have almost no idea what the true value is but the **probability** weighted average of their wild guesses is £2.5 million.

If there is a risk of this misunderstanding taking place then the auditor should point it out. Since giving only **expected values** is poor practice, the obvious recommendation is to provide more information about other possible results.

Second, people might think that 'expected' means 'ought to happen'. Let's imagine the spreadsheet says the **expected** cost of a project is £6.3 million. That means the **probability** weighted average of the guesstimates is £6.3 million. It does not mean that the cost of the project *ought* to be £6.3 million and therefore that's what the budget should be.

Turning **expected values** into budgets or other types of target is a mistake. It is much better to look at the whole **probability distribution** and take a view based on that fuller information.

43   AUDIT POINT: AVOIDING IMPOSSIBLE PROVISIONS

In putting together an initial budget for the 2012 Olympic Games the UK government faced a difficult choice. How much should it include for VAT?

This VAT payment would be a tax paid by the UK government to the UK government, but its inclusion in the budget was still important because funding was not just coming from the general public purse.

Either the games would be declared VAT exempt or they wouldn't. What would you have put in the budget? One perfectly sensible option would have been to budget for the **expected value** of the VAT, i.e. the total VAT bill multiplied by the **probability** of having to pay it at all. How good this is depends on how you value differences between budget and actual, but using the mathematician's favourite, the **expected value** of the budget errors squared, it turns out that the **expected value** for VAT is a great choice.

However, you can imagine that for many people this must have seemed a bizarre choice. It was a budget guaranteed to be wrong. In fact they decided to put nothing in the budget at all and were surprised to find, a year or so later, that VAT would be charged.

44   AUDIT POINT: PROBABILITY IMPACT MATRIX NUMBERS

Here's one that could embarrass a lot of people. Another potential problem with risk register impact and probability ratings comes from the way people sometimes combine them for ranking and selection.

Imagine that the method for combining probability and impact ratings into one rating is defined by the usual grid. Let's say it's a 5 by 5 grid for the sake of argument, looking like Figure 8:

		VL 1	L 2	M 3	H 4	VH 5
P r o b a b i l i t y	5 VH	5	10	15	20	25
	4 H	4	8	12	16	20
	3 M	3	6	9	12	15
	2 L	2	4	6	8	10
	1 VL	1	2	3	4	5

Impact

Figure 8   Probability impact matrix with 25 cells

There are 5 levels of probability ranging from very low (VL) to very high (VH), and the same for impact. The levels have also been given index numbers from 1 to 5. The combined score is found by multiplying the two indices together and is shown in the cells of the matrix.

Oh dear. What people imagine they are doing is taking the **expected value** of the impact, or something like it, but the numbers being used are not probability and impact but the index numbers of the rows and columns.

When you look at the ranges of impact and probability that define each level they are usually of unequal sizes. For example, 'very low' impact might be '£1–1,000', 'low' impact might be '£1,001–10,000', and so on. Typically the levels get much wider each time.

This means that, often, the index numbers are more like the logarithms of the impact and probability so multiplying them gives you something more like 'the logarithm of the impact raised to the power of the logarithm of the probability'! However you look at it, this is a mistake.

What it means is that 'risks' get ranked in the wrong order and if you have a habit of reporting on only 'risks' over a certain rating then the set of 'risks' selected for reporting will usually be the wrong set.

45   VARIANCE

This is a function whose result is often used as **risk**. It is the **expected value** of the square of differences between possible outcome values and the **mean** outcome. That means it gets bigger the more spread out the possible values are.

The way it is calculated depends on what sort of **probability distribution** is involved.

As with other **risk** numbers it is calculated from the **probability distribution** of a **random variable**. For example, if the **random variable** represents the result of rolling a 6-sided die then the **probability** of each of its six discrete outcomes is 1/6 and its **mean** is 3.5 as we have already seen. Its **variance** is:

$$\frac{1}{6} \times (1 - 3.5)^2 + \frac{1}{6} \times (2 - 3.5)^2 + \ldots + \frac{1}{6} \times (6 - 3.5)^2$$
$$= 2\frac{11}{12}$$

Variance can also be calculated for actual data about past events, but this is not **risk**, though it is sometimes taken as an estimate of **risk**, and may be calculated with a slight adjustment in order to be a better estimate.

46   STANDARD DEVIATION

This is just the square root of the **variance**, i.e. multiply the **standard deviation** by itself and you get the **variance**.

As with the **variance**, it gets bigger with more dispersed outcomes.

Also like **variance**, **standard deviation** can be calculated for actual data about past events, but this too is not **risk**, though it is sometimes taken as an estimate of **risk**.

47   SEMI-VARIANCE

A problem with the **variance** and **standard deviation** is that they increase with the *spread* of the **probability distribution**. That means that the possibility of something extremely good happening makes the **risk** number larger. This does not agree with our intuitive idea that **risk** is a bad thing.

the possibility of something extremely good happening makes the risk number larger

Alternative **risk** functions have been invented to try to focus more on the bad outcomes, such as lost money, and one of these is the **semi-variance**.

This is the **expected value** of the squared difference between outcomes below the **mean** and the **mean** itself. In other words, it is the **variance** but ignoring outcomes above the **mean**.

48   DOWNSIDE PROBABILITY

This is another **risk** number that focuses on possible disappointment. It is the **probability** of not getting an outcome better than some target outcome.

What is taken as the target is a free choice and needs to be defined, but could be a target rate of return for an investment, for example. Outcomes better than the target are ignored. The **downside probability** is a function of the target chosen, and will be higher for more ambitious targets.

49   LOWER PARTIAL MOMENT

This combines ideas from the **semi-variance** and the **downside probability**. It is the **expected value** of the squared difference between outcomes below some target or threshold and the target itself.

50   VALUE AT RISK (VAR)

Another **risk** function that focuses on the downside is **value at risk**, and it has become the most famous.

This is calculated as the loss such that the **probability** of things turning out worse is less than or equal to a given **probability** threshold. The **probability** threshold is something that has to be chosen and is usually small.

For example, a bank might model the value change over the next 24 hours of a collection of investments. The loss such that a loss at that level or worse is only 5% likely is their 5%, 1 day **VaR** for that particular portfolio. Put another way, they are 95% confident they won't lose more than the **VaR** over the next 24 hours (see Figure 9).

Like some other **risk** functions, **value at risk** is sensitive to the extremes of a **probability distribution**, which are very difficult to know accurately, and it says nothing about the *very* extreme possibilities. For these and other reasons it has come in for some severe criticism and been cited as contributing to the credit crunch of 2007–2009.

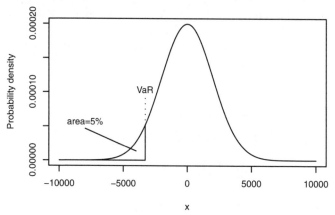

Figure 9 Value at risk based on 5% confidence shown on a probability density function

The name itself is somewhat misleading. It sounds like it represents how much money we currently have invested. A bank might have billions invested but say its **VaR** is just millions. The rest is safe? Hardly.

Value at risk is a common **risk** measure for market risk, i.e. risk related to the value of a portfolio of assets traded on a market (usually a financial market).

VaR is usually calculated on the basis of the market value of the portfolio, not the returns from it (which also include payments such as dividends).

It is usual to assume that the composition of the portfolio is not changed during the period. In reality, trading may well happen during the period so the value of the portfolio will also change for that reason.

It is also common to assume that the **expected** value change of the portfolio during the period is zero. Consequently the only thing that needs to be understood is the variability of market values. **VaR** calculated on this basis is called absolute **VaR**. For periods of just one day this simplifying assumption is not unreasonable in most cases, but for longer periods it may be better to calculate the relative **VaR**, which involves calculating the **expected** market value as well.

Finally, there are alternative bases for calculating market values.

In the chapter on finance we'll look in more detail at how the **probability distributions** used to calculate **VaR** are derived.

51   AUDIT POINT: PROBABILITY TIMES IMPACT

Some years ago I asked a large audience of business continuity managers how they would define 'risk'. The most popular answer was to define it as 'probability times impact'. It is hard to think of a less appropriate definition.

'Probability times impact' is shorthand for the **expected value** of the probability distribution of impact. It is a good candidate for a best guess. It is the number most people would use as an estimate for the impact if forced to give just one number. A risk is something *unexpected*, so 'probability times impact' is the opposite of risk!

More successful ways to define 'risk' in terms of **probability** and impact have held on to the whole distribution rather than reducing it to one number.

The practical problem that 'probability times impact' causes is that outcomes other than the **expected value** get forgotten and uncertainty about those outcomes is ignored, leading to a massive, systematic understatement of **risk**. Business continuity managers should be particularly upset by this because it means that the extreme outcomes they focus on drop out of sight!

Auditors should identify when 'probability times impact' is being used, highlight the problem, and recommend something better.

Table 1 Top ways to go wrong with a risk register

Isolation from the business model
Incoherent mix of mental models
Impossible impact estimates
Undefined situations or events
Focusing on the 'top 10'
Taking risk as probability times impact
Index number multiplication
Confusing money with utility
Ignoring impact spread
Narrow perceptions due to poor calibration and lack of links
between events

SOME TYPES OF PROBABILITY DISTRIBUTION

If you've thoroughly absorbed the contents of the previous chapter then you are already well on your way to enlightenment, but your introduction to the fundamentals of risk mathematics is not quite over.

However, before we plunge into more fundamentals it's time to take a look at some famous types of probability distribution. As always the emphasis will be on building a strong conceptual understanding rather than memorizing or manipulating formulae. During this chapter you will also absorb important ideas about how distributions are shaped and chosen that will be used in later chapters, and you will be introduced to the problem of fat tails.

52 DISCRETE UNIFORM DISTRIBUTION

This **probability mass function** can be used where the **situation** has an **outcome space** with a finite number of outcomes in it. The **discrete uniform distribution** says that the **probability** of each outcome is the same.

Rolling a six-sided die is the classic example, with each outcome having a **probability** of one-sixth.

The **discrete uniform distribution** has just one parameter, which is the **probability** of each outcome.

53 ZIPF DISTRIBUTION

Outside a casino, how often do we find all outcomes are equally likely? Not often. The forces that drive popularity tend to create situations where some things are much more common, and therefore more likely to be encountered, than others. We talk about 'the 80:20 rule', and 'the long tail'.

The **probability distribution** that describes this phenomenon is the **Zipf distribution** (pronounced ziff), which can be applied when the **outcome space** is finite, and sometimes also when it is infinite but countable.

Imagine that the outcomes are put in descending order of popularity (i.e. **probability**) and numbered from 1 up to some bigger number, N. The **probability** of any one of these outcomes, let's call it the *kth* outcome, is:

$$p(k;s,N) = \frac{1/k^s}{\sum_{n=1}^{N} 1/n^s}$$

In this distribution there are two parameters: N, the total number of outcomes, and s, which affects how quickly the **probabilities** drop for less likely outcomes. They stay the same for a particular example of the Zipf distribution while k varies to give the **probability** for each outcome.

Just focus on the top half of the right-hand side, which is a kind of weighting given to each outcome. The weight drops as k increases. For example, in the version where $s = 1$, the **probability** of the second outcome is half that of the first item, the **probability** of the third item is a third of the **probability** of the first item, and so on down the line. If s is bigger than 1 then the **probabilities** drop more quickly.

Outside a casino, how often do we find all outcomes are equally likely? Not often

The stuff under the horizontal line on the right means the sum of the weights of all the outcomes, so that what we are getting is the *kth* outcome's weight as a fraction of the total of all the weights.

Note the way the notation '*p(k;s,N)*' mentions the parameters s and N, but after a semicolon.

54 AUDIT POINT: BENFORD'S LAW

This is a distribution with special appeal for auditors because it has been used to find fraud. Imagine you're a fraudster making up fictitious accounting documents. You have to think of numbers for things like the invoice value and the number in the first line of the address. What numbers should you choose? Obviously you should keep the financial values low enough to avoid detailed scrutiny but high enough to make some decent money. But what numbers exactly?

What most people would not think about is the proportion of numbers that start with each digit. For example, are numbers starting with the digit 1 usually more or less common than numbers starting with 2, or are they equally common?

For numbers distributed logarithmically, which many real world numbers are, the **probability** of starting with the digit d in numbers to the base b (we usually use base 10 but computers are binary and use base 2) is:

$$p(d) = \log_b(d + 1) - \log_b(d)$$

Applying this to numbers in the usual base 10 system, that means that numbers start with a 1 almost twice as often as they start with a 2.

Here's the full data for base 10, showing the percentage of numbers starting with each digit, on average: 1: 30.1%, 2: 17.6%, 3: 12.5%, 4: 9.7%, 5: 7.9%, 6: 6.7%, 7: 5.8%, 8: 5.1%, 9: 4.6%.

Numbers that have been found to conform to Benford's law include electricity bills, share prices, populations of towns, lengths of rivers, and processes described by power laws, like **Zipf distributions**.

The audit test involves thinking through whether the data ought to be distributed according to Benford's law, then checking to see if they are.

55 NON-PARAMETRIC DISTRIBUTIONS

The textbooks are so chock-full of distributions with small numbers of parameters, otherwise known as parametric distributions, that you might think there are no others. Not so.

Non-parametric distributions are useful and can be quite simple to work with once you accept that computer power is needed.

56 ANALYTICAL EXPRESSION

In fact computer power is the key to working with **probabilities** in most practical situations. Many of the **probability distributions** in this chapter have neat-looking formulae, at least for their **probability mass function** or **probability density function**.

These neat formulae, using standard mathematical functions, are called **analytical expressions**. Mathematicians talk about whether there is an 'analytical solution' to problems, by which they mean an **analytical expression**.

Non-parametric distributions do not have neat formulae. They have data tables, and algorithms, so computer power is often needed.

The computer has to represent continuous curves approximately, often by slicing them into hundreds or thousands of tiny pieces, or segments, and repeating calculations over and over. The smaller the pieces, the greater the accuracy, but the longer it takes. In theory this could get slow enough to be impractical but in practice these calculations are almost always done in the blink of an eye.

computer power is the key to working with probabilities in most practical situations

A huge effort has been made over the centuries to find ever more efficient and accurate ways to do the calculations and most quants rely on powerful computer tools to do their work.

Most of these tools focus on number crunching, but there are also tools that can do 'symbolic' mathematics, like we did at school, solving equations, simplifying and expanding expressions, and so on. The abilities of these systems are impressive and early tests of symbolic algebra systems using textbooks revealed many errors in the textbooks!

57   CLOSED FORM (ALSO KNOWN AS A CLOSED FORMULA OR EXPLICIT FORMULA)

A **closed form** is a formula for calculating an answer that provides a definite, predictable end to the calculation. There is no need to search iteratively for the answer, or to evaluate an infinitely long series of sub-formulae, gradually adding more decimal places to the precision of the answer. Often you can work out an answer in a few seconds using a pocket calculator.

Mathematicians also talk about whether there is a **closed form** expression for things. If there isn't then again it is only by computer powered number crunching that the answer can be computed conveniently.

Unfortunately, **closed forms** are few and far between even with the famous **probability density functions**. Sure, they may have a **closed form probability density function**, but that in itself is of little practical use because there isn't a **closed form cumulative probability distribution**. Put it another way, what we usually want to know is **probabilities**, not densities, and **probabilities** come from the area under the density curve, for which there is no neat formula.

58 CATEGORICAL DISTRIBUTION

The **categorical distribution** is a **discrete non-parametric distribution**.

Sometimes the best we can do is to list the outcomes and write a **probability** next to each one. It's not pretty, it's not clever, but it's very useful and very common.

For example, suppose a football team has been selected for a match and we want to write a distribution that shows the **probability** of each player scoring at least one goal.

Clearly, the team members do not have an equal chance of scoring – think of the goalie. We might also know from experience that the **Zipf distribution** does not apply. Combining judgement, the latest results from fitness tests, and some numbers about goals scored in previous matches we could write some semi-judgemental numbers for **probability** against each player's name. That's a discrete **non-parametric distribution** called the **categorical distribution**.

Although this distribution lacks mathematical neatness, a laptop computer can easily process the numbers and help us take our analysis further.

59 BERNOULLI DISTRIBUTION

In the Bernoulli distribution the two outcomes are one and zero, known as 'success' and 'failure'

Take the **categorical distribution** and apply it to a case with only two outcomes and you have the **Bernoulli distribution**.

This is usually counted as a parametric distribution, because really there is only one parameter, which is the **probability** of one of the outcomes occurring. The

probability of the other outcome is just one minus the **probability** of the first.

In the **Bernoulli distribution** the two outcomes are one and zero, known as 'success' and 'failure' respectively. The **probability** of success is nearly always given the name p, though in theory it could be anything. This is one way of writing the **Bernoulli distribution**:

$$Pr(1) = p \text{ and } Pr(0) = 1 - p$$

A **situation** with this **probability distribution** is called a Bernoulli trial and these trials are the building blocks for some very famous parametric distributions.

One of the attractions of these distributions is that it is often easy to see that they will describe whatever it is you are trying to describe simply because it works in the way that matches the theory behind the distribution.

60   BINOMIAL DISTRIBUTION

Suppose we think we have a series of identical, independent Bernoulli trials. For example, we might be thinking of sales made by a telesales person. Each call is a trial. Some calls result in a sale, which is success, but others do not, which is failure.

If we know the **probability** of each single call leading to a sale, what is the **probability** that the caller makes no sales at all in a series of calls? What about making a sale on exactly one call? Two calls? And so on.

This is what the **binomial distribution** is for. Its parameters are the number of trials and the **probability** of success on one trial. It is a **probability mass function**.

If we are interested in the **probability** of exactly k successes from n trials with probability of success of p each time then it is:

$$p(k; n, p) = \frac{n!}{k!(n-k)!} \, p^k (1-p)^{n-k}$$

The exclamation marks in this formula stand for 'factorial'. The factorial of a number is that number multiplied by the factorial of one less than itself. For example, $4! = 4 \times 3 \times 2 \times 1$. Factorials get very big very quickly.

61 POISSON DISTRIBUTION

A distribution that is often used to represent the occurrence of risk events is the **Poisson distribution**.

Suppose the number of trials was very large and unknown. For example, in a large business there are thousands of things happening every day that could go horribly wrong. What if, instead of a telesales person making a few dozen calls, we are interested in a computer processing millions of invoices and worried about the tiny percentage of invoices that are incorrect?

Enter the **Poisson distribution**, which is designed for those **situations** where we have a vast number of trials (theoretically infinite) but the chance of 'success' (in practice we more often think of faults or other risk events) on any one of them is extremely slim.

This is a **probability mass function** that gives the **probability** of getting exactly zero 'successes', exactly one, exactly two, etc. It has one parameter, λ (lambda), and to give the **probability** of exactly k successes it looks like this:

$$p(k; \lambda) = \frac{\lambda^k e^{-\lambda}}{k!}$$

The parameter λ represents the average number of successes overall. The e in this formula is a very special number in mathematics with a fixed value of approximately 2.71828182845904523536 …

The **Poisson distribution** is also good for **situations** where an event might occur an unknown number of times in a given period of time, such as the number of crimes in a town in a week. Obviously this has many uses in risk analysis.

62 MULTINOMIAL DISTRIBUTION

The **binomial distribution** was about what happens when a series of trials is carried out, each having just two outcomes.

The **multinomial distribution** generalizes this to a **situation** where the repeated trials are, again, identical to each other, but this time they have more possible outcomes, with **probabilities** fixed for each one.

For example, if there are three outcomes from each trial – let's call them A, B, and C – and five trials then the multinomial can capture the probability of getting each combination of results, where a combination of results is something like 'A twice, B three times, and C not at all.'

There are plenty more **probability mass functions** to enjoy, but that's enough for this book, so let's go on to something a little smoother and more sophisticated.

63 CONTINUOUS UNIFORM DISTRIBUTION

This **probability density function** can be used with a **continuous random variable** or where the **situation** has an **outcome space** that is a range on a continuous number line.

It says that the **probability** density of every value within a range is the same (see Figure 10).

This means that the **probability** of the outcome being in any sub-range can be calculated very easily.

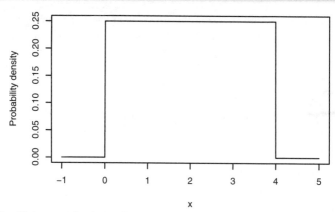

Figure 10 Continuous uniform distribution between zero and four

Situations where we really think that any value is equally likely are not common, but the **continuous uniform distribution** is still important. It's the distribution people often go for when they're not sure they can justify something more informative. If people are arguing then sometimes the easiest thing to do is say, 'Let's just assume they're equally likely'.

64 PARETO DISTRIBUTION AND POWER LAW DISTRIBUTION

To assume equal **probability** is sometimes a good start but few things are equally likely once we have some evidence. Remember the **Zipf distribution**? That was the one that described how popularity often declines when you start with the most popular, go to the next most popular, and so on down the line.

The same phenomenon can be looked at in other ways using continuous distributions. The **Pareto distribution** is named after the Italian economist Vilfredo Pareto (1848–1923) who was interested in how wealth was distributed. He focused on the proportion of people in a very large population whose wealth is above a given number.

The **probability density function** for this gives a **probability** density for each possible level of a wealth, or any other **random variable** of interest, which we'll call x.

$$p(x; k, x_m) = k \frac{x_m^k}{x^{k+1}}, \text{ for } x \geq x_m$$

In this formula x_m is the minimum possible value for the variable and is greater than zero, and k is a positive constant that controls how quickly the curve sweeps down.

This formula is not as complicated as it first appears. What it says is that the **probability** density is proportional to one over the wealth level raised to a power. All the rest is just to get the area under the curve to equal one and make this a valid **probability density function**.

This makes it an example of a **power law distribution** (see Figure 11).

Power law distributions are useful in risk management because they describe quite well the **probability distributions** of events that are usually unimportant but occasionally can be very severe indeed. An example is the severity of stock market crashes.

Power law distributions … describe … events that are usually unimportant but occasionally can be very severe indeed

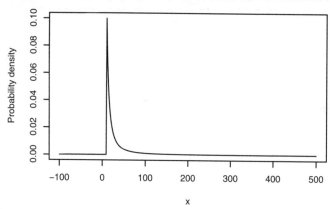

Figure 11 Pareto distribution with $k = 1$ and $x_m = 10$

65 TRIANGULAR DISTRIBUTION

This **probability density function** is also a step up from the **continuous uniform distribution** in that it doesn't regard all possible outcomes as equally likely.

It's the distribution people tend to choose when they've no theoretical reason, or justification from past experience, for choosing any particular distribution, but know that **uniform** is not right. It's a way of saying, 'I don't know what distribution to use so please let's not debate it.'

Notice that this is one of the few **probability density functions** that says extreme outcomes are impossible. That's a good reason for *not* choosing it when you don't know what the distribution type should be (see Figure 12).

The **triangular distribution** has three parameters: a lowest possible outcome, a highest possible outcome, and an outcome somewhere in between that gives the position of the top of the triangle.

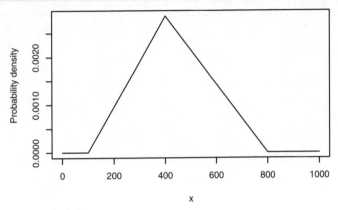

Figure 12 Triangular distribution

Table 2 Good reasons for choosing a distribution type

It was a good fit to similar data in the past
The theory of how the system works matches the thinking behind
the distribution
The distribution is open minded, e.g. fat tails

Triangular distributions are often used in analysing project risks and people are usually asked to give the three parameters for each 'risk' on a list or for each variable in a **model**.

66 NORMAL DISTRIBUTION (ALSO KNOWN AS THE GAUSSIAN DISTRIBUTION)

At last we have arrived at the famous **normal distribution**, otherwise known as the **Gaussian**. (Gauss rhymes with house.) Its associated

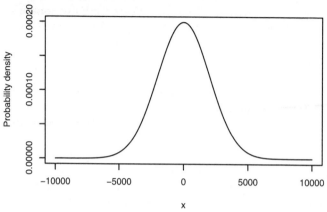

Figure 13 The probability density function of the normal distribution

probability density function is the legendary 'bell curve' (see Figure 13).

As you can see, this **probability density function** is symmetrical about the **mean** and has a 'tail' at each side. These tails go on forever but soon get very thin.

It is in fact similar in shape to a **binomial distribution** for a very large number of trials and the **normal distribution** can be used as an approximation for the **binomial**.

The **normal distribution** has two parameters, μ (myu), the **mean** of the distribution, and σ² (sigma squared), the **variance** but usually written in this way as the **standard deviation** squared.

This distribution is a firm favourite in many areas for two reasons. One is that actual data from several sciences have been shown to be **normally distributed**. The other is that a piece of theory called the central limit theorem says that, with certain strings attached, any large number of distributions *added* together will have a distribution that is **normal**.

Not surprisingly, it is common to assume **normal distributions** are present almost by default, and to stick with that assumption unless statistical tests show that it is clearly not so. If only a few data are available that won't happen.

Risk models used to price securities traded on financial markets have often assumed **normal distributions**. This probably contributed to underestimating the chances of extreme results. There is evidence that the actual tails are often a bit fatter than those of a **normal distribution**.

This doesn't mean there's a mistake in the central limit theorem. It just means that the assumptions it depends on perhaps are not correct for all cases. For example, perhaps their distributions are not independent, perhaps they don't have finite variance, perhaps addition is not involved, and perhaps they aren't all of the same size. There are now other central limit theorems that lead to different distributions, not just the **normal distribution**, when the assumptions are slightly different.

Justifications for distributions based on what would happen if a large number of other distributions were combined in some way are quite common. They are sometimes called 'asymptotic' justifications because they are about what the combined distribution would end up as if we increased the number of contributing distributions infinitely. Keep reminding yourself that in practice you may not be dealing with a large enough number of distributions for the asymptotic distribution to be a good choice, and they may not be combined in the way people think.

Often the most important reason for favouring a particular type of distribution is that it has worked well in the past for similar data. However, even this can be deceptive as different types of distribution can sometimes match the same data equally well.

67   AUDIT POINT: NORMALITY TESTS

A bias towards assuming **normal distributions** is built into the mathematical techniques often used.

Some commonly used mathematical techniques rely on assuming that data are **normally distributed**, or near enough. If that's not true then the techniques don't give the answers they are supposed to.

Checking that the data are **normal** is usually done using normality tests but they don't usually work as you might expect. If the data pass the normality test that does not show they are **normally distributed**. It just shows that the test cannot confidently say they are *not* **normally distributed**.

In short, the typical tests say the data are **normally distributed** unless proven otherwise.

If you have only a few data then they will usually pass the normality test. If you have a ton of data then it is quite common for the data to fail the test even though they are very close to being **normally distributed**.

The tests can also be duped by data that are **normally distributed** in most regions but not in the extreme tails. This is because we have so few data in these extreme regions that comparisons are particularly unreliable.

It is quite possible to have enough data on hand to use a particular mathematical technique, but not enough data to confidently establish that using the technique is appropriate.

Finally, it is sometimes the case that data are **normally distributed** but according to a pattern, and this also indicates a problem with the assumptions.

The validation approach should include looking at appropriate graphs of the data to check for such patterns. Looking at graphs to check **normality** is just about always a good idea.

68   NON-PARAMETRIC CONTINUOUS DISTRIBUTIONS

Just as probability mass functions can be non-parametric, so too can **probability density functions**.

When shown as **probability density function** graphs, these usually look like line drawings of bumpy but rolling hills. You could almost make them by sketching with a pen, and some software actually does let you drag a line with your mouse.

More often they are made by running software over a collection of actual data points. The software draws a line that neatly summarizes and simplifies the shape of distribution the data seem to suggest. It does this by applying a simple formula, which includes a smoothing factor.

---

69   AUDIT POINT: MULTI-MODAL DISTRIBUTIONS

One thing you'll notice about all the famous parametric distributions in this chapter is that they have just one peak, otherwise known as their mode. A real mountain range usually has more than one peak, though some may be higher than others. They are multi-modal.

What about real data? The true distribution of real data can be multi-modal of course, for lots of reasons. If this is the case then a distribution with one mode is unlikely to be a good fit, whatever parameters you choose for it. It's as if the parametric distribution you are trying to use refuses to accept reality.

If an analyst just runs software and uncritically accepts the results then the true situation can be missed. It is important to look at graphs of the underlying data and it can help to fit **non-parametric distributions** to bring out patterns that are hard to see by eye.

70 LOGNORMAL DISTRIBUTION

The **normal distribution** is often appropriate for quantities that are the result of *adding* lots of other distributions. When the quantity is the result of *multiplying* lots of other distributions then the appropriate distribution is more likely to be the **lognormal distribution**.

The **lognormal distribution** is one where the logarithm of values returned by the **random variable** is **normally distributed**. The **lognormal distribution** (see Figure 14) only copes with values for the variable above zero.

The parameters are μ (myu), the **mean** of the natural logarithm of values returned by the **random variable,** and σ (sigma), the **standard deviation** of the natural logarithm of values returned by the **random variable**. That means that μ and σ don't give you the **expected value** and **standard deviation** of the distribution, though formulae for these are available.

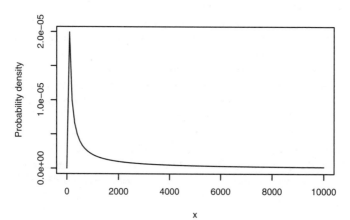

Figure 14 A lognormal distribution

71   AUDIT POINT: THIN TAILS

Looking back at the last few figures in this book you can see that all the distributions tail off towards the right. This tail looks like it gets very thin, and often it does. However, some tails are thinner than others.

For example, the tails of a **normal distribution** are much thinner than the tails of a **power law distribution**.

The tails are all about events that are rare, but extreme when they do happen. That means it is often hard to decide which curve to use because there are so few data on very rare events.

72   JOINT DISTRIBUTION

So far, all the distributions have been for one **random variable**. Often it is more accurate to consider variables together.

For example, suppose we want to describe the **probability distribution** of newborn baby weights and lengths.

Weight will have a distribution. Length will have a distribution. However, weight and length are related. On the whole, longer babies will also tend to be heavier.

Rather than use a **probability density function** to show the distribution of weight, and another to show the distribution of length, what we really need is a distribution that shows the **probability** density for any combination of weight and length.

This is what **joint distributions** are for. They can also have more than two variables, e.g. weight, length and temperature.

Working with **joint distributions** greatly increases the computer power needed to arrive at answers, but is usually unavoidable.

73   JOINT NORMAL DISTRIBUTION

As an example of a **joint distribution**, here's the two dimensional **joint normal distribution**, which really is bell shaped, at least when the distributions are nicely matched and independent of each other (see Figure 15). This is not the case for the weights and lengths of babies, which are linked.

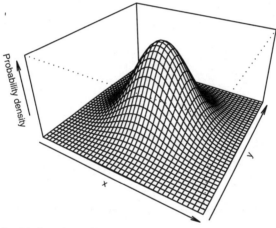

Figure 15   Normal distribution in two variables

74   BETA DISTRIBUTION

The **beta distribution** is one of my favourites. It's got two good things going for it. First, by choosing different values for its two parameters it is possible to put it into an amazing variety of shapes. Second, it is a really simple way to show your current views about success/failure rates.

The **beta distribution** covers the range from 0 to 1, or 0% to 100% if you prefer (see Figure 16).

Figure 18 illustrates the **beta distribution** in action.

> *Beta distribution ... is a really simple way to show your current views about success/failure rates*

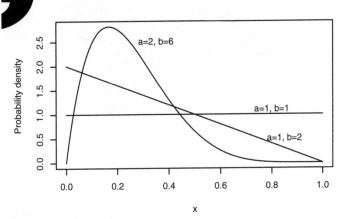

Figure 16   Beta distribution with various values for the two parameters

AUDITING THE DESIGN OF BUSINESS PREDICTION MODELS

If you've stayed focused so far your mind will already be well on its way to some staggering new powers. You are ready to pick up vaguely worded risks and silly calculations with probability impact matrices. You know that talk of the unconditional probability of something is probably misguided.

You can also understand some quite sophisticated jargon. For example, suppose a risk quant says something like 'Our model of event occurrence is basically Poisson and back-testing shows it's well calibrated.' You can take this in calmly, knowing that the Poisson distribution is a typical choice for the number of risk events in a period of time, and that calibration is just a measure of how well the probabilities match up to reality. You might also think to ask if they have any information about resolution.

However, there is still much more to learn. This next chapter is about business prediction models – indeed any attempt to predict the future. You'll find these coming from the finance department, arising in business cases for projects and other investments, in pricing models, capital adequacy and solvency models, and elsewhere.

Often business prediction models don't mention risk or probability but in most cases they should

Often business prediction models don't mention **risk** or **probability** but in most cases they *should*; the fact that they don't is a major weakness that so often leads to risk being ignored or underestimated and to all the stress, crises, missed opportunities, and disappointment this usually brings.

This chapter is also about models because understanding what mathematical models are and what they are made of is the key to understanding the mathematical approach to risk management and makes a lot of others things very clear.

Let's get started.

75   PROCESS (ALSO KNOWN AS A SYSTEM)

In the last chapter we began with the simple idea of a **situation** with possible outcomes. Most attempts at prediction are aimed at the behaviour of a **system** or **process** that generates a series of outcomes falling within the definitions of one or more **situations**.

The **process/system** might be a machine in a factory, a sales force, a marketing website, a gang of criminals up to no good, a team of nurses at work, a rabbit warren – really anything we choose to define in these terms.

76   POPULATION

A **process** results in a series of outcomes that can build up to create a large **population** of outcomes (e.g. baby rabbits, thefts, healthy people), though it might not be large.

For example, the sales force of a company produces a stream of sales. From the point of view of an external auditor interested in the results of a specific accounting year, the set of sales that should be included in the year is a **population** of great interest. Subsets of that **population** will be studied in order to form an opinion about the whole **population**, and this information will be combined with other evidence about the behaviour of the **process** that generated the **population**. From the point of view of an *internal* auditor it is the performance of the **process** that is more likely to be the main interest.

77 MATHEMATICAL MODEL

Mathematical models are models in the same way that a toy train set or a scale model of the Eiffel Tower made out of matchsticks is a model. They are smaller, cheaper, more convenient representations of the real thing.

Mathematical models are often useful for making predictions about the future, ideally what the future might be like if we followed possible courses of action.

Mathematical models can be of a **process** or a **population**. They range from the simplest model, such as a single number representing the average or spread of a **population**, to something much more ambitious, like a model that represents individually each of thousands of work items flowing around a factory.

Our minds make use of many types of mental model, and **mathematical models** tend to be among the most clearly defined of these models.

A **mathematical model** is made of mathematical objects, put together with varying degrees of skill and knowledge in an attempt to represent the world in a useful way.

The ability to make reliable predictions is particularly prized

It's good if **mathematical models** closely match the reality they represent especially when we want to know what would happen if we took different courses of action. The ability to make reliable predictions is particularly prized.

Models are also designed with ease of use in mind. It is perfectly sensible to have more than one model of the same **system** or **population** if they are designed to be used for different purposes.

An important point to understand about **mathematical models** used in risk analysis is that they don't usually represent 'risks'.

Mathematical models represent the whole relevant system, not just some 'risks', and it is uncertainty attached to values in the model, expressed using **probability distributions**, that is where 'risk' is involved.

---

78   AUDIT POINT: MIXING MODELS AND REGISTERS

People sometimes think that **mathematical models** can be slotted under a risk register to provide more detail behind risk ratings. In truth, **mathematical models** are fundamentally different in concept from the disembodied 'risks' appearing on risk registers and this idea of just providing more detail is wrong.

The **mathematical model** should be the main representation and if a list of things is needed then that list can be made by running through objects in the model and listing the **risk** associated with each one.

---

79   PROBABILISTIC MODELS (ALSO KNOWN AS STOCHASTIC MODELS OR STATISTICAL MODELS)

Some **models** include one or more **random variables**. That makes them **probabilistic models**. Very often they are acting as **probabilistic forecasters**, making their predictions in probabilistic terms. For example, rather than predicting success the model gives a **probability** for success. And rather than predicting next month's sales it gives a **probability distribution** for next month's sales.

This is much better in principle than just making a prediction of the outcome, usually on a 'best guess' basis. The **probabilities** convey more information and help people keep an open mind.

If the **probabilities** actually represent just **long run relative frequencies** then there is more uncertainty to be expressed. It may be clearer to use the phrase 'estimated frequency' instead of 'probability' and also disclose uncertainty about the frequencies in terms of **probability**.

This is a very important point to understand so here is a typical problem that illustrates the varieties of prediction. Imagine we are studying the work of an invoicing clerk who produces invoices in batches of ten. We have checked *some* of the last batch. Here are some facts about the clerk's performance we might want to forecast in some way:

- The total value of the errors in the last batch.
- The total value of the errors in some specific future batch.
- The **long run relative frequency** distribution of the total value of errors we would get if we checked a huge (infinite) number of batches in the future and summarized our results.

It may be clearer to use the phrase 'estimated frequency' instead of 'probability'

In this example I've chosen to focus on the total value of the errors in a batch, but it could have been some other statistic about errors in the batch, such as how many of them there were, or what their average value was, or how many were made on pink paper.

Forecasts that give no information about our uncertainty about these facts would be, respectively:

- A best guess for the total value of the errors in the last batch (taking into account what we know from the items checked so far and the scope for more problems in the remaining batch items.
- A best guess for the total value of the errors in some specific future batch.

- A chosen distribution type along with best guesses for the values of parameters of that distribution type.

These are not good forecasts. Note that, although the last forecast is 'probabilistic' in the sense that it uses **probabilities**, these represent only **long run relative frequencies** so important uncertainty is not being presented.

Forecasts that present uncertainty better would be, respectively:

- A **probability distribution** for the total value of errors in the last batch.
- A **probability distribution** for the total value of errors in some specified future batch.
- A chosen distribution type along with a **probability distribution** for the values of parameters of that distribution.

80   MODEL STRUCTURE

Mathematical models consist of mathematical objects, like variables, linked to each other by other mathematical objects, such as functions and relations, often expressed as equations.

In a **mathematical model** these objects are given names. Usually, these names are just single letters from the English or ancient Greek alphabet, but some styles of mathematics use whole words to make the names easier to remember.

Documents describing **mathematical models** often introduce them with lots of sentences starting with words like 'Let V be...' and may contain formulae described as assumptions, definitions, or axioms.

Some bits of this text do nothing more than give names to things. Other bits make assumptions that could be wrong. It can be very difficult to distinguish the two types.

81 AUDIT POINT: LOST ASSUMPTIONS

Documents introducing **mathematical models** often make no attempt to separate statements, just introducing notation from statements that make assumptions that could be wrong. Perhaps it is because the writer thinks predictions will be the true test of the model and worrying about assumptions is unnecessary. Clearly assumptions do matter, especially when we have few data on predictive reliability, so not highlighting the assumptions clearly is a dangerous omission.

This could be the start of a pattern of behaviour that leads to people losing track of the assumptions and not doing enough to consider when they are unsafe. The 2007–2009 credit crunch was partly caused by over-reliance on a formula for valuing collateralized debt obligations whose assumptions had been stretched to the limit and beyond.

Auditors should check that assumptions are clearly identified and their reasonableness is considered at appropriate points.

82 PREDICTION FORMULAE

A **mathematical model** just represents a **population** or a **system**. It makes statements about what the **population** is like, or how the **system** can behave.

To actually make a prediction from a **mathematical model** often requires a bit more work. Sometimes it is possible to deduce a formula that spits out the numbers you want to predict. This I'll call a **prediction formula**.

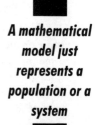

A mathematical model just represents a population or a system

83   SIMULATIONS

Some **mathematical models** are able to represent a **system** at a particular point in time or stage in its life, and show how the **system** then moves from one state into the next, and into the next, and so on as time passes, or as a sequence of events unfolds. This is a **simulation**. It's like a chain of predictions.

84   OPTIMIZATION

Some **mathematical models** allow repeated predictions about what would happen if different courses of action were taken, and using these and an appropriate search strategy it is sometimes possible to find good courses of action.

Sometimes it is even possible to find what people claim to be the **optimum** course of action, but this is just within the confines of the **model**. In reality there is nearly always something you could do differently, making room for creativity.

85   MODEL INPUTS

Most predictions based on **models** are like functions; you give them some input values and they give you back one or more predicted results.

In the case of **simulations**, you give the **prediction formula** the state of the **system** at a particular point in time and it tells you what the next state will be, and the one after that, and so on.

This means that the predictions can be wrong simply because the **input** values you gave are wrong. Some **prediction formulae** are extremely sensitive to slight errors in **inputs**.

For example, **simulations** used to predict the weather are given thousands of pieces of data about air pressure, temperature, and other aspects of the weather across a wide area, sometimes the whole world, and then they simulate the atmosphere and show the future weather the **model** thinks is most likely given that starting point.

Giving one of these **models** even very slightly different **input** values will produce a weather prediction that starts off similarly but soon begins to diverge from the original prediction. Since the **input** values are taken from many different devices and other sources, and any number of them could be wrong, or slightly inaccurate, or just rounded to the nearest tenth of a degree, incorrect weather predictions could arise because the **input** data are imperfect.

predictions can be wrong simply because the input values you gave are wrong

(This kind of sensitivity to initial conditions is associated with chaos theory, and afflicts even some completely deterministic mathematical systems.)

Today, weather modellers increasingly run their models a number of times with the inputs changed just a bit to see how sensitive the predictions are to changes in input values. This is called ensemble forecasting. They find that the predictability of the weather varies.

86 PREDICTION FORMULA STRUCTURE

As with a **mathematical model**, a **prediction formula** contains objects such as variables that are then connected together.

However, the difference is that in a **prediction formula** some of those variables are **inputs** and some are outputs.

Connecting the **inputs** to the outputs are any number of bits and pieces, including intermediate variables and functions. Buried within these functions will be more Greek/English letters, but some of these represent numbers called parameters. (We have already met parameters, but here is some more information about them.)

Parameters are thought of as fixed numbers, even though a lot of calculation and analysis is often involved in working out what values to give them.

A simple **model** known as Hooke's law illustrates the ideas. For elastic materials (e.g. springs not stretched too far) it relates the force exerted by the spring to the amount that the spring has been stretched.

Robert Hooke (1635–1703), a British physicist, originally wrote the law as an anagram in Latin, 'ceiiinosssttuv' which he later unravelled as 'ut tensio, sic vis' meaning 'as the extension, so the force.' Even if you don't like mathematics very much I hope you can see that the following formula is easier to cope with than a dodgy anagram in Latin:

$$F = -kx$$

where F is the force exerted, x is the extension of the spring beyond its normal resting length, and k is a parameter specific to the spring in question (otherwise known as a 'constant').

The k and the x are written side by side with no symbol in between. In this context that means they are multiplied together, but in mathematics things are not always consistent.

This equation is the model (and they don't come much simpler) and two **prediction formulae** are possible. One tells you the force, F, given the extension x, and looks exactly like the model. The other tells you the extension, x, assuming you know the force. It looks like this:

$$x = \frac{-F}{k}$$

The parameter k is something that usually has to be found by measuring the actual spring when it is stretched by a known force. Once you've done that for one force the **prediction formulae** can be used for any force or degree of extension, at least within limits.

87   NUMERICAL EQUATION SOLVING

It isn't always possible to deduce a **prediction formula**. Sometimes the closest we can get is an equation, deduced from the **model**, that is true for just certain special values of the variables, but which can't be rearranged to produce a convenient **prediction formula**.

Those special values that satisfy the equation are the predictions we want, but without a simple formula how can we find them? The answer is to use numerical methods, which are very efficient trial-and-error methods that iteratively search for the best solutions and quickly close in on them.

Numerical methods have become very sophisticated since the invention of the computer. Before that it was only mathematicians with extraordinary patience or amazing mental calculation skills, such as Alexander Craig Aitken (1895–1967), who were in a position to contribute.

(Just to give you some inkling of Aitken's incredible abilities: he could recite the first 1,000 digits of π (pi) at a rate of 50 digits every 15 seconds. He could work out 1/697 in his head. He could work out 123×456 in about a second, including checking it.)

If you've ever used the Solver add-in on Microsoft's Excel application then you've seen numerical methods at work.

Where a prediction is derived by equation solving there are usually still **inputs** to supply in order to get the desired output.

88   PREDICTION ALGORITHM

It's not uncommon for probability calculations to magnify the slight limitations of digital arithmetic

In fact most predictions, whether using a **prediction formula** or relying on **numerical equation solving**, involve using a computer to calculate the final numbers.

This **prediction algorithm** is the final stage at which things can go wrong, with plenty of scope for coding mistakes and rounding problems. It's not uncommon for **probability** calculations to magnify the slight limitations of digital arithmetic on an ordinary computer.

89   PREDICTION ERRORS

As mentioned earlier, it is nice if a **model** leads to predictions that are reliable. Getting to that happy situation is rarely easy and many things contribute to the **prediction errors**.

90   MODEL UNCERTAINTY

We usually do not know exactly how inaccurate our **model** is. This overall **model uncertainty** has a number of causes, including these:

- **Model** structure uncertainty, which comes from the possibility that the structure of the model is wrong in some way.
- **Model** parameter uncertainty, which comes from the possibility that the parameter values we have chosen are not the best.
- Numerical approximation uncertainty, which comes about because we (1) cannot calculate with actual numbers to complete accuracy

in every case and (2) sometimes have to find solutions by a sort of hunting strategy that does not guarantee that the very best answer will be found.

91 AUDIT POINT: IGNORING MODEL UNCERTAINTY

Model uncertainty is an uncomfortable subject and can be technically challenging, so it's not surprising that people tend to shy away from it.

When I was a teenager I watched *Star Trek* on television (the original series). Each week the crew of the *Enterprise* would get into a perilous situation, often because randy Captain Kirk had done something impulsive. They would then be forced to take an extremely dangerous course of action, at which point Science Officer Spock, a Vulcan famed for his command of logic, would sometimes say something like 'Captain, the odds against surviving are 1,233.5 to one, approximately.'

At the time I thought this quite impressive, but thinking about it later I realized something was not quite right. Despite these long odds against surviving they always did. Where had Spock gone wrong?

Clearly, he had ignored **model uncertainty**. A better way to state his claim would have been to make at least some disclosures about **model uncertainty**. For example, 'Captain, assuming I've understood our situation correctly, the structure of my model is correct, the parameters I have assumed are correct, and measurements are correct, then the odds against surviving are 1,233.5 to one, approximately.'

With these qualifications we can more easily appreciate what a waste of breath his contribution was in these difficult moments. To my recollection Kirk never changed his approach in response to Spock's calculations of the odds, so perhaps they had agreed to skip the **model uncertainty** disclosures!

In real life, if **model uncertainty** is being ignored it is a problem and the auditor should raise it.

92　MEASUREMENT UNCERTAINTY

Another source of **prediction errors** is using incorrect **input** values. **Input** values are based on measurements and measurements are not necessarily correct. This is the problem of **measurement uncertainty**.

93　AUDIT POINT: IGNORING MEASUREMENT UNCERTAINTY

Measurement uncertainty is with us all the time and yet often ignored, with unpleasant practical consequences.

The person in the street might imagine that audited financial accounts are correct and so the **measurement uncertainty** is zero.

What accountants and others in the know appreciate is that many of the numbers are just one version the auditors would have accepted, and that's even before we get into deliberate false accounting.

A lot of accounting is driven by estimates and the auditors will accept a range of estimates that seem to them defensible. These estimates include things like the useful life of machinery, the value of debts that should be provided against because of the risk of non-payment, and the market value of securities for which there isn't a liquid market.

Most 'information' reported in organizations is a lot less reliable than audited accounts. It includes things like customer satisfaction figures, derived by asking questions of a small selection of customers whose views can vary even with irrelevant factors like the weather.

Quality measures based on people double-checking items looking for faults can be unreliable because they almost never spot *all* the faults.

Measurement uncertainty can often be reduced and sometimes that is worth the investment. It is always important to disclose **measurement uncertainty** in some way so that people using data know their limitations.

I have seen examples of leading companies that acted for months on the basis of internally produced data that were grossly incorrect but presented without comment.

94 AUDIT POINT: BEST GUESS FORECASTS

Many forecasts used in business, perhaps most, are a best guess about the value of a number in the future.

Our natural tendency is to think too narrowly about the future, to believe our forecasts are more accurate than they really are, and to believe we have more control of events than we really do have. Best guess forecasts tend to exacerbate this illusion.

We need to be reminded that predictions can be wrong and that means making suitable disclosures and giving some information about how accurate the prediction is likely to be. Just rounding numbers is not an adequate answer to this challenge.

Failing to explain the limitations of forecasts is a serious weakness in managing risk and auditors should identify it and recommend providing more information about the uncertainties involved.

95 PREDICTION INTERVALS

Is there a way to start to understand the **model uncertainty** of a **mathematical model**? Yes. In fact there are two basic approaches.

The simplest approach to understand and do, if it's possible, is to compare predictions with what actually happened.

This may take a long time if we have to wait to discover the actual outcome each time, but often it is possible to use historical records and compare what our **model** *would* have predicted with what actually happened.

If the prediction is probabilistic then this is estimating **calibration**.

The subject of comparing models to reality is a large one and covered at length in the next chapter.

This approach to **model uncertainty** has the advantage of being a true test against reality, but the disadvantages are that (a) it does not directly tell us what contributed to the total **model uncertainty** so we can reduce it, and (b) it only tests against reality so far, ignoring the possibility of being surprised by something new.

If the predictions are on a best guess basis then the pattern of prediction errors can be used to add some rough and ready **prediction intervals** to the prediction.

For example, the best guess forecast of sales next month might be £301,000. However, using data about past forecasting errors we might be able to add that there is a 10% chance of sales being higher than £354,000 and a 10% chance of sales being lower than £245,000. These two sales values give a prediction interval. Put another way, we are 80% sure the actual sales will be within that range. (You don't have to use these percentages.)

People tend to see **prediction intervals** as very solid, precise information so they must be used carefully, especially when forecasting methods are changed and past performance is less of a guide to current accuracy.

96 PROPAGATING UNCERTAINTY

The other basic approach to exploring **model uncertainty** is to analyse the uncertainties that feed into the **model** and **propagate uncertainty** to the predictions. This shows what our various input uncertainties imply about the uncertainty in our predictions.

This is useful in the many **situations** where comparing predictions with actual results is not possible, e.g. long-range climate forecasts. It also requires us to think about **events** that have never happened before.

As an illustration, imagine you are the boss of your own business, selling ice cream on a beach during summer. Each day you take a stock of ice cream out in your van and sell as much as you can.

For the sake of a simple explanation let's just imagine that you sell only one product, a delicious organic peach and vanilla flavoured Cornish-style ice cream scooped into a cone and topped with fruit coulis. It's yummy but how does your turnover vary with demand?

Your prediction of daily sales is that your sales are based on demand, except when you run out of stock. In a more mathematical style:

$$S = P_s \times \min(U_D, U_I)$$

where S is the value of sales on a day, P_s is the sale price per unit, U_D is the demand in units on the day, and U_I is the stock (inventory) taken out on the day. The function min() gives the lowest value out of U_D and U_I, which means that you don't sell more than your stock.

You could just put in your best guesses for each of the inputs, P, U_D, and U_I and get a single estimate for S. You could, but you shouldn't.

These inputs are all uncertain to some extent, especially the units of demand. What does this uncertainty mean for your prediction about sales?

The idea behind **propagating uncertainty** is to find out what un-certainty around **inputs** and other aspects of a model implies for the uncertainty of the prediction. Over the coming pages you will learn how this can be done.

97 AUDIT POINT: THE FLAW OF AVERAGES

Many people think they can ignore their uncertainty in **models** like this because, surely, if they use their best guess for all the **inputs** then the prediction will also be a best guess. Actually no, not unless the **model** is 'linear' and most people don't even know if their **model** is linear or not. Professor Sam Savage has coined the marvellous name, the *flaw of averages*, to highlight this problem.

The ice cream **model** above is not linear because sales are capped by the limited ice cream stock.

Suppose your best guess for sales demand on a Bank Holiday Monday is £500 but from one year to the next there are big variations so you judge that it is possible to achieve sales as high as £850 with unlimited stock, or as low as £150 if the weather is poor.

If you take stock with a sales value of £700 out in the van and the sales demand is below this then sales demand will contribute fully to the **expected** sales figure. However, if sales demand is more than £700 then sales will still be £700 only. Those exceptionally good possibilities will not contribute fully to your **expected** sales figure.

This means that the **expected** sales figure will be below the level it would be if stock was not limited. This is the impact of uncertain demand combined with the non-linearity of the stock limit.

The flaw of averages usually leads to overestimates of value.

If no attempt has been made to **propagate uncertainty** through a **model** then auditors should ask if business modellers are aware of the flaw of averages and if they have checked if their **model** is linear or not. The error could be large.

98   RANDOM

To understand the simplest and most widely used method of **propagating uncertainty** you need to know a bit about **randomness** first.

The meaning of **random** has been debated for a very long time and some interesting perspectives have emerged. Let's begin with some of the qualities we associate with **randomness**.

Last year my children went through a period of describing things as 'random', as in 'Yeah, the teacher went mad and just gave us **random** homework.'

In this example I'm sure the teacher would dispute that the homework was **random**, but from the boys' point of view the choice of homework was something that seemed haphazard, without pattern, and was inexplicable. In other words, it was **random**.

This example has two elements that are commonly found. There is a **process** (the one by which the teacher selects the homework) and an output from that process (the homework itself). The idea of **randomness** can be applied to both the **process** and its outputs (i.e. the **population** of data resulting).

Processes that are **random** tend to be finely balanced and it is often the case that the outcome is the result of a huge number of factors. We think of coin tossing, roulette wheel spinning, shuffled decks of cards, and radioactive decay. We do not think of voters, car engines, or computer programs.

Outputs that seem random to us lack patterns we can see

Outputs that seem **random** to us lack patterns we can see. For example, the sequence to coin tossing results 'HHHHHHHH' doesn't seem as **random** as 'HHTHTHTT' even though each is just as likely to occur. A battery of mathematical tests has been invented to check if data are truly **random**. These work

by searching for different kinds of pattern that might be present. Of course they don't guarantee there is no pattern; they just confirm that the patterns they look for are not present.

99   THEORETICALLY RANDOM

Where is **randomness** found? The place it can be found in abundance is in **mathematical models**. If a **model** includes a **probability distribution** then the values it provides are assumed to have the perfect **random** qualities of true **randomness** by definition. The real **situation** the distribution is modelling may be anything but **random**, but the element in the **model** is beautifully, perfectly, reassuringly **random**.

For example, people buying and selling securities on a large market do so deliberately, for good reasons. They would say their behaviour is not **random**. Nevertheless, **models** of the prices of securities almost always assume that price movements are **random**. Sometimes those **models** even make good predictions, so representing non-random processes with **probability distributions** isn't necessarily wrong.

100 REAL LIFE RANDOM

Does **randomness** exist anywhere in the real world? Opinions have differed, but as our understanding of causality has improved the scope for **randomness** seems to have shrunk. We now know that even completely deterministic systems can be impossible to predict because their changes over time may be finely balanced on details.

Some say that **randomness** exists in reality at the sub-atomic level and that this has been proved by quantum theory.

I take this with a pinch of salt, bearing in mind that this same quantum theory says that a cat in a box may be neither alive nor dead until the moment we open the box and take a look, precipitating reality into choosing one or other fate for the cat.

---

101 AUDIT POINT: FOOLED BY RANDOMNESS (1)

It is common to think that one thing caused something else when in fact it did not, and it was really a combination of other factors, acting together in ways we did not understand, that produced the result. (This collection of other factors is labelled 'randomness' even if it is not truly **random**.)

For example, suppose a school buys a software program designed to help students learn new spellings. To test the program one set of students uses the program for a month and another set does not. At the end of the month they all take the same spelling test and happily the ones who used the new software do better.

Money well spent? Probably, but spelling test scores are influenced by lots of things. A student might be distracted by romantic thoughts, recovering from a virus, still angry from a fight at break time, or perhaps feeling brainy after listening to some classical music. And what if the words selected for the test just happened to be the ones some children had difficulty with?

If students took spelling tests every day their scores would vary from test to test for all these reasons and more. Occasionally they would produce great scores and occasionally they would be terrible. Mostly they would be somewhere in between.

If several students in the set that used the software were having a good test and several of the other students were having a bad one then that could have been the reason for their different average scores. It might have been nothing to do with the software.

Another example is that professional investors with higher-than-average success often think this is due to their skill. It might not be. After all, investment results differ and so some people are going to be above average and some below.

Here's a way to get a reputation as a fortune teller. Write to 4,096 people telling them the FTSE 100 index will end higher tomorrow and to another 4,096 people saying it will be lower. The next day 4,096 people know you were right and 4,096 know you were wrong. Forget the ones who think you were wrong and divide the others into two groups of 2,048. Write to them in the same way about the next day of trading and soon you will have 2,048 people who know you were right both times. Split them and repeat the procedure, over and over.

After 10 waves of letters you will have 8 people who think your powers of prediction are uncanny because you've been right 10 times in a row. They've been fooled by **randomness**.

102 AUDIT POINT: FOOLED BY RANDOMNESS (2)

There is another way to be fooled by **randomness** and it's probably just as common. In this mistake we fail to understand something and conclude that it is **random** and therefore *cannot* be explained or predicted. As a result we stop trying when a bit more effort might have been rewarded with quite good predictions.

Mathematical methods sometimes encourage this mistake by using the phrase 'random error' to refer to the difference between a model's predictions and reality. Consequently, the quant sets up the **model**, tweaks it to give the best predictions of available data, and declares the rest 'random error', wrongly implying that better prediction is impossible. Similarly, the term **random variable** encourages us to see phenomena as **random** even when we have no evidence that they are.

Some outcomes are unpredictable just because we don't yet know how. Others are unpredictable given the information we choose to consider. Others are unpredictable even given all the information we have. In all these cases there is still a chance to do better.

There are also other outcomes that are unpredictable given all the information it would be feasible to gather. Perhaps, and philosophers and scientists are still arguing, there are also outcomes that are unpredictable given *full* information because they are truly **random**.

103 PSEUDO RANDOM NUMBER GENERATION

It is very useful (for reasons I'll explain soon) to have a supply of **random** numbers, or a way to generate new **random** numbers on demand.

Open up Microsoft's Excel program and enter the formula '=RAND()' into a cell. You will see a number between zero and one. Now press the F9 key to make the spreadsheet recalculate and you will see another number replace the first, again something between zero and one.

The Help system will tell you that this function gives a **random** number. This is not quite true. What it gives is successive numbers from a completely fixed sequence, generated by repeatedly applying a mathematical formula. If you knew the formula and found the right starting place you could predict each new number exactly.

Having said that, these numbers do look haphazard and they pass many of those **randomness** tests because they are free from a lot of common patterns.

What Excel is doing is **pseudo random number generation**. Happily, these numbers are **random** enough for many practical purposes and very convenient. This is a great example of a non-random process that generates very **random** looking output.

Although '=RAND()' gives numbers evenly distributed between zero and one it is possible to get **pseudo random number generation** to spit out numbers to match just about any **probability distribution** we want, over any range.

104 MONTE CARLO SIMULATION

The simplest and most popular method for **propagating uncertainty** through **models,** and so exploring **model uncertainty** without the benefit of comparisons with real outcomes, is **Monte Carlo simulation**. The ability to generate numbers at **random** to match a **probability distribution** is the key to **Monte Carlo simulation**.

The name **Monte Carlo simulation** seems to suggest to many people a technique that is complicated, probably expensive and difficult to do, and that only people with large domed foreheads should attempt.

Ironically it is just the opposite. **Monte Carlo simulation** takes away complicated mathematical reasoning and replaces it with a very simple technique that requires only a huge amount of repetition – done for us by a computer at the click of a button.

A child can do it, can understand it, and can afford it. Today's laptop computers are so powerful that they can do it really well, and very quickly, even with quite complicated **models**.

To explain how it works let's go back to the ice cream sales **model**:

$$S = P_s \times \min (U_D, U_I)$$

This says that sales are equal to selling price times the lower of units of demand and units of stock.

Now, let's assume that the **Monte Carlo simulation** is being done the usual way, using an Excel add-in. The ice cream sales **model** will be set up initially on the spreadsheet as if to use best guesses, with cells into which you would normally type values for **inputs** (P_S, U_D, and U_I).

However, instead of typing values in we choose a **probability distribution** for each of the **inputs** for which there is some significant uncertainty. In this case the sales price and stock levels are choices rather than estimates, and the relationship between sales, price and volume is pretty solid, so it is only the units of demand, U_D, that are uncertain.

Some tools give more help with selecting **probability distributions** than others. The best ones let you see a graph of the curves you are working with, and give helpful feedback numbers so you can pick a **distribution** that nicely reflects your uncertainty about the true value.

When this is done the **model** has been given **input** values or a **probability distribution** (indicating **degrees of belief**) for every **input** or parameter.

The next step is to pick the cell whose value is the output, the daily sales, and tell the tool how many simulations to do. A reasonable choice would be 10,000. Click to start.

What the **Monte Carlo simulation** tool then does, 10,000 times, is this:

1 Use **pseudo random number generation** to select values for each uncertain **input** according to the **probability distributions** you specified.
2 Calculate the output value using the spreadsheet **model** as usual.

3 Collect the output value and store it.

Having done this it summarizes the output values it collected, ready to show graphs and statistics of different kinds that you might ask for (see Figures 17(a)–(d)).

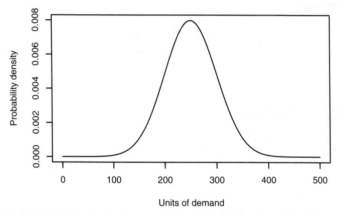

Figure 17 (a) **Probability distribution** representing **degrees of belief** that each possible level for units of demand is the true one

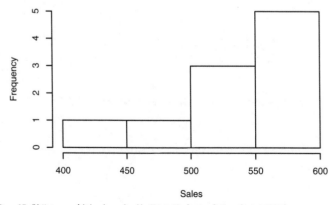

Figure 17 (b) Histogram of daily sales produced by **Monte Carlo simulation** after just 10 trials

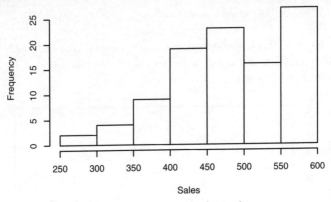

Figure 17   (c) Histogram of daily sales after 100 trials. Can you see what it is yet?

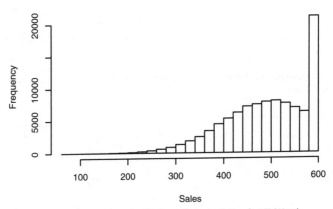

Figure 17   (d) Histogram of daily sales produced by **Monte Carlo simulation** after 100,000 trials

105 AUDIT POINT: IGNORING REAL OPTIONS

Another common problem that can result in significant mistakes in valuing projects and other investments is the failure to value our ability to react to information we receive in future.

Obviously reacting to new information is something we do all the time and it has a big impact on the results we achieve. Typically it improves the value of what we do.

Unfortunately, generations of accountants have been trained to make spreadsheet **models** on the basis that everything has to be decided up front.

For this reason their valuations will tend to be too low, though not by a predictable amount and there is no guarantee that it will compensate for the overestimate caused by the flaw of averages!

It is possible to include reactions to new information in a decision tree but, if you are using **Monte Carlo simulation**, it is easier and more informative to build them into spreadsheet simulations.

For example, if you have a model that shows the position in successive periods (e.g. months) you can insert a formula using the 'IF()' function to check values at the end of a month and set up a value in the next month that reflects a decision policy.

Many of these decisions could, theoretically, be taken at any time and modelling such situations can be difficult. However, people are rarely vigilant enough to take the decision at any time so it is probably more realistic to insert a decision into the **model** only at points where people might realistically take a decision.

106 TORNADO DIAGRAM

Which of the uncertain **inputs** to a **model** contribute most to uncertainty in the outputs? One way to get a feel for that is to calculate how closely variations of each **input** seem to be linked to variations in the outputs.

When this information is plotted on a graph in the usual style it is called a **tornado diagram** because the picture looks a bit like a tornado. The **input** whose uncertainty contributes most is shown first by a horizontal bar, and then the others are shown beneath it in order of decreasing importance, with the bars getting shorter each time.

Take a moment to consider how great this is. We built a model of how various things, some we choose and some we don't, contribute to a result we care about. Then we expressed our uncertainty about their values. The **Monte Carlo simulation** then worked out how our various uncertainties feed through to a prediction about the result we are interested in. And, finally, it showed us which uncertainties are most important.

when we ask people to shout out 'risks' in a workshop ... what we get is a muddle

In short, we did a risk analysis. However, instead of a jumbled list of badly defined sentences thrown together in a workshop, we used variables structured into a clearly defined mental model. And instead of relying on some kind of intuition to guess the ultimate impact of various things that could happen we captured the things we knew most easily, and then let our **model** and the software tool work out the rest.

This tells us a lot about the nature of risk analysis. It is true that danger exists in our lives and that there are some things that are inherently difficult or even impossible to predict. However, it is not true to say that 'risks' exist in the real world outside our thinking.

We live in a fog of uncertainty. Mental models, with their associated uncertainty, are our main way of structuring that fog so that we can understand it, identify changes, and make decisions. When we derive a list of uncertainties from a **model** they are structured, linked, and relatively well defined. We can see that we have a complete analysis with respect to our **model**. In contrast, when we ask people to shout

out 'risks' in a workshop we get uncertainties from the mental models of many people but cut off from those models, then phrased in the format of 'risks'. In short, what we get is a muddle, though it may be rich in potentially interesting clues.

Monte Carlo simulation is very commonly used in analysing the schedule and cost risks of large projects.

---

107 AUDIT POINT: GUESSING IMPACT

It's quite common for risk management procedures using risk registers to ask people to give estimates of 'impact' that are far too difficult to give.

Sometimes there is no problem. Some potential problems, if they occur, have easily identified consequences that can immediately be turned into money. For example, if an invoice is not paid then the impact is the value of the invoice. If a car is stolen then the cost is whatever the insurance doesn't cover, and perhaps more expensive insurance in future.

However, many items on many risk registers have far more wide-ranging consequences that are hard to imagine let alone estimate. For example, what is the impact of a fraud perpetrated by a director? There will be money lost, of course, but also a great deal of credibility, leading to various consequences for raising money, recruitment, and sales, to list just the obvious ones. The effects may be long lasting and may combine with each other.

How can a human's intuition directly assess all this and give a reliable estimate of 'impact'? It can't and it is dangerous to think it can.

The auditor can check items on risk registers to see if the estimates of impact can reasonably be given directly. If not, then some kind of numerical modelling, or other aid to thinking through knock-on effects, can be recommended.

108 CONDITIONAL DEPENDENCE AND INDEPENDENCE

In real life, once one thing starts to go pear-shaped it often drags a lot of other things down with it

Outcomes are often connected to each other in such a way that the **probability distribution** of one depends on the value of another, or several.

For example, the impact of an explosion might depend on the size of a fuel leak, among other things. The length of a baby is linked to its weight, so if you know a baby's length then your expectations about its weight should change. These variables are **conditionally dependent** on each other.

If **random variables** are not connected in this way then they are **conditionally independent**.

Conditional dependence is inconvenient. It makes it harder to build the models. Not surprisingly, people often prefer to assume independence. In the litany of assumptions made to introduce a **model** you will often see the abbreviation 'iid', which is short for 'independent and identically distributed'.

In analysing risk it is important to consider **conditional dependence** very carefully. If variables in your **model** are dependent, as they often should be in practice, the risks shown by the **model** will usually be much *larger* than if you assume independence. In real life, once one thing starts to go pear-shaped it often drags a lot of other things down with it, giving you the full fruit bowl.

109 CORRELATION (ALSO KNOWN AS LINEAR CORRELATION)

One of the most common ways to express the connection between two variables is using a **correlation** number.

Correlations vary between 1 and –1. A **correlation** of 1 means that the two variables are perfectly positively **correlated**; when one is big, so is the other, and the relationship is completely regular and predictable. A **correlation** of –1 means the two variables are perfectly negatively **correlated**, so when one is big, the other is small, and the relationship is completely regular. A **correlation** of zero means there is no connection between them, at least not of the kind captured by **correlation** numbers.

With any decent **Monte Carlo simulation** tool you can specify the **correlations** between uncertain inputs and the **pseudo random number generation** it does will take those **correlations** into account and generate numbers with the required **correlations**, or thereabouts.

In effect, what is happening is that you are giving a **probability distribution** for each variable on its own, and a table of **correlations**, and then the tool is turning that information into a **joint probability distribution** for all the variables together.

However, using **correlations** gives only a very limited range of shapes for the **joint probability distribution**.

110 COPULAS

The idea behind **copulas** is to provide a method of generating a much wider variety of **joint probability distributions** from the separate **probability distributions** of each individual variable.

There are several types of **copula** and each has its own parameters.

Copulas are used for a wide range of purposes in mathematical modelling, especially in finance. However, there are yet more methods for generating dependent values from **random variables**.

111 RESAMPLING

If you already have a lot of real data that reflect the **conditional dependence** between two variables (e.g. the length and weight of many babies) then you can use them in **Monte Carlo simulation**. Simply select babies in your database at random over and over again and use their values for length and weight. This means you won't explore any situation that hasn't happened before, but at least it captures the statistical link between the variables quite well.

112 CAUSAL MODELLING

Why are the values of variables **correlated** at all? Presumably it is because, somewhere along the line, they are connected by causality. Either they influence each other or they share a driver at some point.

A good way to capture **conditional dependence** is often to represent the causal links in the **model**. Sometimes it is easier to make estimates of causal links than to estimate **correlation** numbers.

In summary, the main techniques for capturing conditional dependence are correlations, copulas, resampling, and causal modelling.

113 LATIN HYPERCUBE

Monte Carlo simulation has its drawbacks. One of them is that it sometimes takes a lot of trials to get accurate results and a few **models** take a long time to run just once, let alone thousands of times.

Weather **models** take so long to run that the 50 or 100 runs done for 'ensemble forecasting' (their name for **Monte Carlo simulation**) are an impressive feat of computer power.

In particular, rare combinations of events happen rarely in the **Monte Carlo simulation** trials, just as they do in real life. To get accurate results in the extreme tails can involve running a huge number of trials.

Various tricks have been invented to get around this. The best known is the **Latin hypercube**, which is a method of choosing values for inputs more systematically so that coverage is more evenly spread.

114 REGRESSION

A misleading, but common, explanation of **regression** is that it is a technique for *finding* associations between variables. It is not. It is just **modelling** in yet another guise.

A more interesting definition says it involves fitting a **probability distribution** of the variable(s) to be predicted, given different possible values for the variables from which the prediction is to be made.

For example, suppose we want to predict the cost of invoicing mistakes in a month and believe it rises with the number of new customers taken on in the month. Our **model** will be one that gives a different **probability distribution** for the cost of invoicing mistakes for each possible level of new customers.

Not only would we like these distributions to be well **calibrated**, but we would also like them to be **sharp**. Usually this means that the distributions are narrow and vary a lot with conditions.

In the next chapter we'll look at a common problem with **regression** that may have grown out of the idea that it is for *finding* associations.

*A misleading ... explanation of regression is that it is a technique for **finding** associations between variables. It is not*

115 DYNAMIC MODELS

It's time to move on to another aspect of **mathematical modelling**: time.

A convenient assumption to make is that a **process** is unchanging over time – it's just the same **situation** repeating over and over again. Having made this assumption we use data generated by the **process** over a period of time as if it reflects unchanging characteristics

This is convenient, but rarely correct. **Processes** change and so there are also **models** that try to capture the change, and to interpret historical data as the result of a changing **process**.

There are many mathematical techniques for modelling time series (i.e. data showing behaviour over time).

116 MOVING AVERAGE

Given a series of data over time, one way to predict what will happen next is to calculate an average of the last few data points. For example, if you have weekly sales figures for the last two years and want to predict next week's sales you could take the average of the past four weeks, or some other number of weeks.

In practice this would not be a very smart choice as seasonal factors usually need to be taken into account. However, it illustrates the idea of taking the average of recent data, also known as the **moving average**.

One of the interesting things about **moving averages** is what good predictors they tend to be in a variety of applications. Intuitively, they shouldn't be so good, but they are, particularly the exponential **moving average**, which is calculated by weighting each past data point so that older data are progressively less important to the prediction.

AUDITING MODEL FITTING AND VALIDATION

The previous chapter introduced a lot of ideas about building models and exploring uncertainty about how true to life they are.

However, it left out two of the biggest and most important topics, which are (1) how models are adjusted to fit reality using past data, and (2) how models can be tested against reality to assess how far they can be relied on.

These tasks are very different in principle, but are taken together because in practice they involve similar ideas and data, and are done at virtually the same time.

To understand the issues involved, and the techniques available, we need to step back and spend some time looking at a new set of fundamental ideas.

These are ideas that have been living in my head since they jumped in from a book in the library of University College London more than 20 years ago. They've been there so long it's hard to imagine what it would be like without them, but I recall that they seemed stunning at the time and greatly changed my views about science, learning, and beliefs.

One of your rewards for carefully reading this chapter will be the ability to spot some increasingly subtle but still devastating mistakes. For example, imagine a friend of a friend comes to you and enthusiastically explains his exciting discovery:

I've found a way to make money by betting on the outcomes of league football matches. It's amazing. I've been number crunching through years of past results and by fitting a probit model using stepwise regression I've found some variables that predict results better than the bookmakers and they're highly significant statistically. And look, I've even done simulations showing that, if I'd used my system over the last few years, I would have made a healthy profit. Do you want to get in on the action?

The clues are there and as you read this chapter I hope you will see the problem. We'll return to this at the end of the chapter and you can see if you were right.

117 EXHAUSTIVE, MUTUALLY EXCLUSIVE HYPOTHESES

If you dimly remember something about 'hypothesis testing' from a course on statistics, don't even try to remember more of it. This is not about hypothesis testing, but about something much more powerful and useful.

This is about getting closer to the truth when more than one possible explanation exists. For example, an auditor might see some loan documents that are missing signatures. Is it fraud? It might be, or perhaps it isn't.

This is about getting closer to the truth when more than one possible explanation exists

The true situation can be analysed in powerful ways if the alternative explanations (i.e. hypotheses) are exhaustive and mutually exclusive.

For example, with those missing signatures, the hypotheses could be 'It's fraud' and 'It's not fraud.' It must be one of these, logically, so that makes them exhaustive. It's also impossible for them both to be true, making them mutually exclusive.

In that example there were just two hypotheses, but there can be more and often the number is infinite. For example, suppose we are given a bent coin and want to know the **long run relative frequency** of heads if it is tossed in the usual vigorous way.

The true **long run relative frequency** of heads could be anywhere from zero to one and every possible level is another hypothesis. Together they cover all the possibilities for this value and they are mutually exclusive.

The possible explanations could be alternative **models**, or at least the same **model** structure with different parameter values. We might be trying to find the best **model**, or at least the best **model** parameters for a given structure. In the latter case the hypothesis is not that we have the best **model** possible, but that we have the closest **model** given a particular structure. Better **models** could exist with different structures.

118 PROBABILITIES APPLIED TO ALTERNATIVE HYPOTHESES

Where we have multiple **exhaustive, mutually exclusive hypotheses** we can show how likely we think it is that each is true using a **probability function**.

Linking this back to **probability interpretations**, you can think of the hypotheses as statements that each might be true. Alternatively, you could say that the **situation** is one where we find the true explanation (i.e. the best hypothesis) and the **outcome space** includes all the explanations we are considering (i.e. the set of **exhaustive, mutually exclusive hypotheses**).

Usually, the **probability function** shows the view held at a certain point in time, or on the basis of certain items of evidence.

119   COMBINING EVIDENCE

In a typical problem where we are trying to focus on the true explanation from a number of alternatives we start with some evidence, and that gives us a view as to the **probability** of each hypothesis being true.

Then we get more evidence and, as a result, revise our opinions.

Philosophers may argue about whether we are ever in a situation with no evidence at all, and about what to do in those situations (if they exist).

In practice we always have some idea, even if it's just gut feeling, perhaps informed by eons of evolution. And, if we can't agree on where to start, we can also choose the start from an initial **probability distribution** that is as open minded as possible.

In a typical problem where we are trying to focus on the true explanation from a number of alternatives we start with some evidence

120   PRIOR PROBABILITIES

When we're considering the impact of a piece of evidence the **probabilities** attached to each hypothesis before the evidence is considered are called the **prior probabilities**.

121   POSTERIOR PROBABILITIES

And the **probabilities** attached to each hypothesis after the evidence is considered are called the **posterior probabilities**.

Of course these **posterior probabilities** could then become **prior probabilities** in the next round of evidence processing.

122 BAYES'S THEOREM

A very famous formula links **prior probabilities** and **posterior probabilities** and it is attributed to the Reverend Thomas Bayes (1702–1761), a Presbyterian minister with interests in God and logic. This is not only a useful formula but the word Bayesian denotes a whole approach to what **probability** means and how to use it.

Most people who are taught a bit of statistics as part of a science course at school or university are not taught the Bayesian approach. That's a pity because it is easier to understand, increasingly dominant in applications of **probability** theory, and very useful.

Table 3 Some famous Bayesians

Thomas Bayes
Pierre-Simon Laplace
Alan Turing
John Maynard Keynes
Howard Raiffa
Bruno de Finetti
Frank Ramsey
LJ Savage
Harold Jeffreys
Edwin Jaynes
Arnold Zellner
Dennis V Lindley

> *Bayes's theorem ... tells us how much we should believe in each hypothesis after considering some new evidence*

What is Bayesianism? It's what you've been reading for the last few pages. Keep going and you'll soon have the basics mastered.

Bayes's theorem uses the notation of **conditional probabilities** and tells us how much we should believe in each hypothesis after considering some new evidence, given our initial views. In the simplest form it says:

$$Pr(H \mid D) = \frac{Pr(D \mid H) . Pr(H)}{Pr(D)}$$

Where:

- H represents a particular hypothesis;
- D represents the data observed (i.e. the new evidence);
- $Pr(H|D)$ means the **probability** that this particular hypothesis is true given the data we are now considering (i.e. the **posterior probability**);
- $Pr(D|H)$ means the **probability** of the data occurring as they did assuming the hypothesis is true;
- $Pr(H)$ is the **probability** we had for the hypothesis being true before considering the data (i.e. the **prior probability**); and
- $Pr(D)$ is the **probability** of the data we saw actually occurring, which is usually calculated by adding the **probabilities** of the data given each hypothesis taken in turn.

To find our view on each of the possible hypotheses this formula has to be applied to each one of them.

One of the advantages of the Bayesian approach is that it has explicit **prior probabilities**. The main alternative methods have **prior probabilities** as implicit assumptions built into the statistical method. You aren't aware of their influence, you can't change them, and you can't combine evidence from more than one source. Although it may take a bit of thought to select appropriate **prior probabilities**, it is a mistake to say that requiring **prior probabilities** is a problem with Bayesian methods.

123 MODEL FITTING

Mathematical models and **prediction formulae** usually contain parameters whose value needs to be chosen in some way.

The most important way to do this is to get hold of some real data about the **population** or the behaviour of the **system** in the past and prefer values for the parameters in the **model** that produce predictions close to past actual data. This is **model fitting**.

Now here's a crucial point. Think back a few pages to the bit about **exhaustive, mutually exclusive hypotheses**. Every possible **model**, including every possible combination of values for **model** parameters, is an alternative hypothesis for the best **model** possible (or the best possible for a given **model** structure).

Past data is evidence and we can **combine that evidence** in arriving at our views on what **model** structure(s) to use and what **model** parameter values to use.

Here is the simplest example. Suppose we have a very bent coin and we want to make a **probabilistic model** that gives the **long run relative frequency** of heads.

In our **model** there is just one parameter to choose, and it's the number for the **long run relative frequency** of heads. What value(s) should we use?

At first, when we haven't tried flipping the coin at all, we have high uncertainty about the **long run relative frequency** of heads. We toss the coin once and it comes up heads. Does that mean it always does? No, but at least we've eliminated the possibility that it never comes up heads, and our evidence actually tells us that higher proportions of heads are now more likely than lower proportions.

The sequence of graphs in Figure 18 illustrates this idea. The **probability distribution** used is a **beta distribution**.

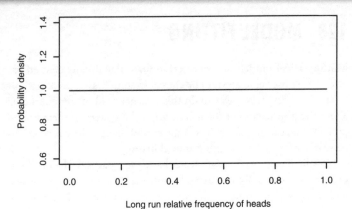

Long run relative frequency of heads

Figure 18 (a) **Prior probability** density function starts off uniform, for the sake of argument

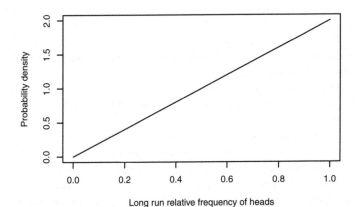

Long run relative frequency of heads

Figure 18 (b) **Posterior probability** density function after one flip of the coin, coming up heads

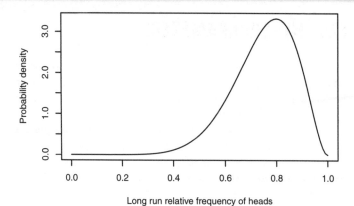

Figure 18 (c) **Posterior probability** density function after flipping 8 heads and 2 tails

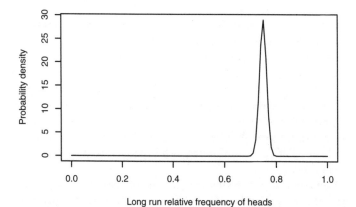

Figure 18 (d) **Posterior probability** density function after flipping 749 heads and 251 tails

124 HYPERPARAMETERS

In the example of the bent coin (Figure 18) the parameter we wanted to find was the proportion of heads, and we gradually closed in on it as the data came in. The **beta distribution** was used to capture the **prior** and **posterior probabilities**.

The **beta distribution** itself has two parameters that determine its shape, alpha and beta. Obviously there is scope for getting confused between the parameters in the problem. To avoid this, parameters of **prior** and **posterior distributions** (alpha and beta in the example) are called **hyperparameters**.

125 CONJUGATE DISTRIBUTIONS

Often there are some simple circumstances where an **analytical expression** can be used to capture the **probabilities** involved, but beyond that we must turn to computer systems using numerical methods and brute force.

The neat formulae use a discovery called **conjugate distributions**.

When using **Bayes's theorem** for **fitting models** there are two types of **probability distribution** involved: (1) the distributions of **prior** and **posterior probabilities**, and (2) the distribution that gives the **probability** of the data assuming each hypothesis is true (often called the likelihood function).

Conjugate distributions are pairings of these two distribution types that have a lovely property. This property is that the **prior** and **posterior distributions** can be the same type, but with slightly different parameter values.

Usually, the type of the likelihood function is given by your **model**, so it's a matter of choosing a conjugate prior from those available for that likelihood function.

For example, it can be shown that if the likelihood function is a **Bernoulli distribution** then the **conjugate distribution** to use for the **prior probabilities** is the **Beta distribution**. The **posterior distribution** will also be a **beta distribution** but with slightly different parameter values that are easy to work out using **closed form** expressions.

There are conjugate priors for a range of common likelihood functions (including the **normal distribution**, **Pareto distribution**, **uniform distribution**, and **Poisson distribution**).

When **conjugate distributions** can be applied the number crunching needed is drastically reduced.

If these are not available then it's back to numerical methods involving processing thousands of sample items and trying to converge on a solution.

Provided there aren't more than about 10 parameters in the **model** it is feasible to cover the possible bundles of parameter values systematically. Beyond that, more sophisticated simulation methods are usually used. The best known of these use varieties of 'Markov Chain Monte Carlo', which is quite sophisticated and usually done with special software.

Remember that the output from these calculations is a **probability distribution** over all possible combinations of values for the model's parameters. Hopefully this will peak nicely to show where the best parameter values are located.

However, at any point in time we remain at least a tiny bit uncertain about what is truly the best bundle of parameter values, so we still seem to have a problem: how to decide which to use.

There are some alternative ways to make that choice, but before I mention some of them I should point out that making a choice isn't necessary and isn't usually the ideal approach. There are at least two alternatives.

126 BAYESIAN MODEL AVERAGING

The idea behind this is that we don't have to pick just one set of **model** parameters, or even just one **model** structure. If we take the Bayesian approach of applying **probabilities** to alternative hypotheses then evidence will give us a **probability distribution** over all the possible hypotheses.

But, instead of choosing one hypothesis and making predictions with it, we can take the predictions from each and every hypothesis and combine them by taking a **probability** weighted average of their predictions. The **probability** used for weighting is the **probability** of each hypothesis being the best one.

It's a lot of number crunching, but if it's done by a computer you probably don't care. **Bayesian model averaging** can often give better predictions than just picking one best **model** from all the possibles and it gives better information about the reliability of its predictions.

127 AUDIT POINT: BEST VERSUS TRUE EXPLANATION

Overall, Bayesianism promotes good management of risk because it keeps our minds open to more hypotheses (i.e. alternative explanations) and so to more possible futures.

However, there is one logical limitation people need to be aware of: it helps select the best explanation from those considered, which is not necessarily the best overall or the true explanation.

In particular, even if an analysis considers all possible values for model parameters, it may be that a model of a different form would be a better one.

128 HYPOTHESIS TESTING

A more widely known (but not better) approach is to make inferences about the best hypothesis without necessarily coming to a specific choice. If you took a course in statistics as part of a science degree this is probably what you were taught.

Let's go back to the example of the spelling software and use it to illustrate hypothesis testing. Recall that the value of some new software for teaching spellings was tested by having one group of students use it while another did not, then comparing their spelling test results.

In this comparison the students who used the software scored a little better in the test, but was that due to the software or just because of a combination of other factors?

The first step in the **hypothesis testing** approach is to nominate a 'null hypothesis'. In comparisons like this the null hypothesis is traditionally that there is in fact no difference in spelling skill between the two groups of students.

The next step is to make some assumptions about the variability of spelling ability, typically using the scores as a guide.

The next step is to calculate the **probability** of getting the difference observed, or a greater one, assuming the null hypothesis is true and in fact the spelling software makes no real difference.

The final step is to compare the calculated **probability** with some criterion such as 5%. If the chances of getting the actual results are less than the criterion then the difference is called 'significant' and the null hypothesis is rejected, implying that the software makes at least some difference. If the calculated **probability** is greater than 5% then the null hypothesis keeps its crown and stays in place.

Although this procedure still dominates many areas of science it has little to offer the practical risk manager.

Suppose the procedure shows that the impact of the software is 'significant' at the 5% level (i.e. the **probability** of getting at least that rise in spelling scores assuming the software actually doesn't give an advantage is less than 5%). So what? What we want to know is *how much* difference it makes. All the **hypothesis testing** tells us is that it makes some difference. Unfortunately, the word 'significant' tends to suggest the difference is 'big' too, which isn't necessarily true.

The other glaring problem is that the null hypothesis seems to get an unfair advantage. What if the teachers all agree that the spelling software is well designed and gives the students a lot more practice than they would usually get? A priori they have a good feeling that the software helps and the trial seems to confirm it. But what if the difference did not prove to be statistically significant? Concluding that the software makes no difference and abandoning it seems madness.

A less obvious point is that the statistical claim is not what most people think. It says that the **probability** of getting the difference seen, or more, assuming the null hypothesis is true, is less than some arbitrary level, traditionally 5%. What people tend to think it means is that there is less than a 5% chance that the null hypothesis is true given the difference observed. Unfortunately, it does not mean that or imply it.

In contrast, using the Bayesian idea of assigning **probabilities** to all hypotheses means it is possible to make statements about the **probability** of the null hypothesis being false, if you want to.

129   AUDIT POINT: HYPOTHESIS TESTING IN BUSINESS

If you see someone outside a scientific paper use **hypothesis testing** statistics you should be suspicious immediately.

If they refer to getting 'significant' results check that the meaning of this has been made clear and nobody has made the mistake of thinking that 'significant' means 'big' or 'worthwhile'. If they decide to keep the null hypothesis then check that a potentially important difference has not been overlooked.

130 MAXIMUM A POSTERIORI ESTIMATION (MAP)

Having discussed two approaches to **model** fitting that do not involve picking one set of parameter values it is now time to look at some techniques that do.

One simple idea is to pick the hypothesis (i.e. the bundle of parameter values) currently thought to be the most likely to be the best. This is the **MAP**.

The **MAP** is based on the **probability** of each hypothesis being true, given the data. This is what is shown by **posterior probabilities**.

131 MEAN A POSTERIORI ESTIMATION

While picking the hypothesis (i.e. bundle of parameter values) that currently seems most likely makes a lot of intuitive sense, there can be problems.

What if the **probability distribution** of the parameters is ragged, so that there is more than one peak to its graph? By eye you might see that there are several peaks near to each other and probably the best estimate is going to be somewhere near the middle of that region.

For this reason, a better estimate is usually to take the **expected value** (i.e. **mean**) of the **posterior distribution**. This is much more suited to a Bayesian style, with its emphasis on using the whole distribution.

This estimate will also minimize the **expected value** of the square of the differences between the estimated parameters and all other possible values, weighted using their **probability** of being true. This is known as the mean squared error and minimizing it is a popular and traditional goal.

132 MEDIAN A POSTERIORI ESTIMATION

Yet another approach is to take the median of the **posterior distribution** of **probabilities** of hypotheses being correct.

133 MAXIMUM LIKELIHOOD ESTIMATION (MLE)

The **MLE** technique sounds like it's going to be the same as **maximum a posteriori estimation (MAP)**, but it's not, even if it sometimes gives the same answer. The **MLE** is based on the **probability** of the data being seen given each hypothesis, which is the other way around to the **MAP** we looked at earlier.

In this respect **MLE** is counter intuitive, just like **hypothesis testing**. Incidentally, it owes a lot of its fame to the same person, Sir Ronald Aylmer Fisher (1890–1962), who was interested in statistics for farming research and genetics.

(Fisher and his supporters were remarkably successful in promoting their ideas on how statistics should be done, but the bruising battle for dominance created personal animosities that can still be seen operating today. His life story is an extraordinary reminder of how attitudes have changed in the last 80 years. He was an ardent supporter of eugenics, and for a time was Professor of Eugenics at University College London. His strong statements on the differences between people of different races would have been seen as racist today. When he was 27 years old he married a girl just days after her 17th birthday, in secret, knowing her parents would not approve. A smoker and a consultant to tobacco firms, he denied the correlation between smoking and lung cancer.)

As it happens, if you thought all rival hypotheses were equally likely before you considered the data then your **MAP** selection will be the same as your **MLE** selection. If you're keen then you can check back to **Bayes's theorem** to see why.

Like the **MAP**, **MLE** suffers from the problem of dealing with ragged distributions.

Also, because it involves picking one possible set of values for the parameters and ignoring other possibilities, it tends to understate uncertainty.

This point is illustrated by Figure 19, which shows the difference between using best guesses for parameter values and using **Bayesian model averaging** with a uniform prior. To create this graph a set of 50 randomly distributed data were generated to simulate some real data with an unknown distribution. Then different quantities of these data were used as the basis for two quite different approaches to fitting a **normal distribution** to the data. In one approach a best guess was

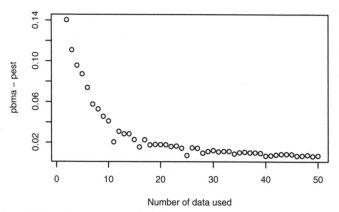

Figure 19 Difference between **Bayesian model averaging** and taking the best parameter values assuming a uniform prior distribution

made for the **mean** and **standard distribution**. In the other approach **Bayes's theorem** was used to create a complete posterior distribution for the **mean** and **standard deviation**.

Then both approaches were used to estimate the **probability** of the next value from this source being below a given, rather low value. This might represent, for example, the **probability** of making a loss of more than a certain amount. The difference between the two **probabilities** is what you see in Figure 19, labelled 'pbma – pest'.

The best estimate is narrow minded about the possible underlying distribution of the data, whereas the **Bayesian model averaging** approach, which started with an assumed **uniform continuous distribution** as a prior, is more open minded and gives a higher **probability** of more extreme results.

When only a small number of data points is used the difference between the **Bayesian model averaging** and the best guess approach is large, but as more data are used the difference is reduced.

Do not imagine that once you have 40 or 50 data points to work with the difference can always be ignored. In this example the difference is very small, but if the **model** was more complex, with more parameters, it would have taken more data to settle down.

The understatement of uncertainty resulting from taking a best guess at parameter values is mitigated if the best guess is presented as an estimate of a **probability** (interpreted in the **long run relative frequency** sense) and accompanied by error bands of some kind.

134 AUDIT POINT: BEST ESTIMATES OF PARAMETERS

Making some kind of best estimate for parameter values is extremely common and usually involves **maximum likelihood estimation**. These estimates always ignore some uncertainty and sometimes it is important. (However, this is mitigated if the estimate is accompanied by suitable error bands.)

It is easy for an auditor to establish if best estimates are being used but hard for the auditor to know if the uncertainty ignored was important, particularly where the quants have done nothing to check.

The obvious recommendation is to do something to check the extent of uncertainty lost by relying on best estimates. This might be covered by work to compare a model's predictions with reality. Alternatively, it could be done (as in Figure 19) by doing a Bayesian analysis to get the full distributions across parameters then using **Bayesian model averaging** to see how much difference it makes.

135 ESTIMATORS

MLE is an idea that was originally developed to deal with very simple **model fitting** requirements, typically trying to work out the **mean** of a distribution. In this simple context it is usually called an **estimator**.

Estimation theory covers the ideas involved in designing and selecting **estimators** for parameters of distributions using real data. An unbiased **estimator** is one that, on average, is right rather than having a tendency to be too high or too low.

Perhaps surprisingly, many well-known **estimators** are biased, and the bias is greater when there are few data.

Another oddity with the well-known **estimators** is that they usually estimate one parameter at a time. So, for example, if you want to fit a **normal distribution** and need to estimate the **mean** and **standard**

deviation, each of these estimates is done with its own separate formula.

If you want to know how reliable the estimate of the **mean** is then there is a simple formula for that, but you need to know the **standard deviation**. Of course, you don't know the **standard deviation** so you have to estimate it from the data. How reliable is that estimate and how does that unreliability affect the estimate of reliability of the estimate of the **mean**? Awkward. This style of estimation is far more complicated than it seems at first.

In contrast, the more sophisticated approaches take possible values of the **mean** and **standard deviation** together. Conceptually this is simpler and more comprehensive.

Figure 20 illustrates this using a simple numerical approximation. After considering just one data point certain combinations of **mean** and **standard deviation** already seem to stand out from the crowd, though this impression is partly caused by the way the graphing software scales the data to fill a standard box. The apparently flat plain around the sharp mountain still has quite a lot of **probability** under it. Given more data the distribution is broader looking but in fact the

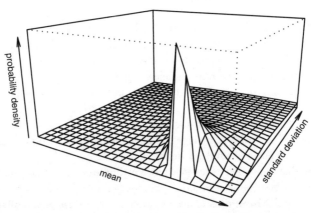

Figure 20 (a) Fitting two parameters simultaneously. **Posterior distribution** after 1 data item is used

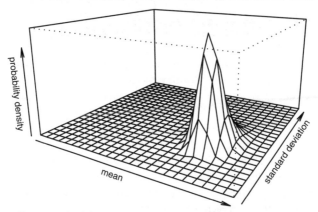

Figure 20 (b) Now appears broader but closer to the true values after using 10 data points

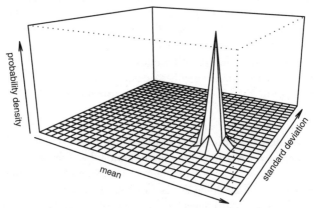

Figure 20 (c) Tighter again with 50 data points used as evidence

'flat' plain is considerably lower and the peak is much higher. With 50 data points used the distribution has tightened visibly around the true values and that flat plain really is very low indeed.

136   SAMPLING DISTRIBUTION

When an estimate is made, how can we assess its likely accuracy? If we have a full **posterior distribution** for the parameter(s) in question it is possible to make a number of statements about other possible values. This is perhaps the ideal situation.

However, if the estimation method is less comprehensive and relies on a simple formula an alternative is to think about the **sampling distribution**. The idea is that the current estimate is made on the basis of data that is just a subset of a much larger **population**. If we took many other samples from that **population**, at **random**, and calculated the **estimator** from each of them, the distribution of those estimates is the **sampling distribution**.

For example, if we are trying to estimate the **mean** of a distribution from a number of data points the usual approach is to calculate the **standard deviation** of the **sampling distribution** of the **mean** of the samples. This is known as the standard error.

Assuming the **sampling distribution** is **normal**, the standard error lets us calculate bands on either side of our estimate and say we are confident to a specified degree that the true **mean** lies between the bands. This is called a confidence interval.

Unfortunately, there is a Catch-22 in this because in order to deduce the **standard deviation** of the **sampling distribution** we need to know the **standard deviation** of the **population**. Obviously, in most cases we don't know it (we don't even know the **mean** of the **population**, which is why we are doing the data analysis). Consequently we have to estimate the **standard deviation** from the data we have.

137   LEAST SQUARES FITTING

In the Bayesian scheme of things we have a **model** with structure and some parameters. The set of parameter values that gives a **model** best fitting the **system** is what we are often trying to close in on and as data are processed the analysis begins to show which values for the parameters are more likely to be the best choice.

With a full **probability distribution** to peruse we are in the luxurious position of being able to choose between such techniques as picking the most likely hypothesis and using **Bayesian model averaging**. If anyone is interested we can show exactly how confident we are about what parameter values to use. In other words, we can say a lot about **model uncertainty**.

However, if your schooling was anything like mine, all this seems rather unfamiliar and you are perhaps wondering where **least squares fitting** slots into this scheme.

Least squares fitting, you may remember, is the technique based on adding up the square of each difference between a data point and the predicted value for that data given by the **model**. The goal is to find the parameter values that minimize the total of the squared differences. This is the traditional approach to fitting a straight line through some data, but it can be used with lots of other **models**.

as data are processed the analysis begins to show which values for the parameters are more likely to be the best choice

This method tells us one set of parameter values is the best one, assuming that the differences are **normally distributed**, using a **maximum likelihood** basis (or assuming we had no prior views and rely entirely on the data).

The thinking behind this is that the **model** will not fit the data perfectly because of influences not captured in the **model**, but which we can ignore because they are **random**, and probably also **normally distributed**. They are usually imagined to be irrelevant measurement errors.

Clearly there are some convenient assumptions at work here and some or all of them could be wrong. The differences between reality and the **model** might be more than just measurement errors and they might not be **normally distributed**.

In simple cases there are **closed form** expressions that give parameter values from data, but more generally software is needed to hunt around for the parameter values that give the **least squares fit**, or near to it.

138 ROBUST ESTIMATORS

robustness ... refers to techniques that give reasonably good answers even when assumptions are not met very closely

A lot of early theorizing about **estimators** was focused on estimating numbers given a number of attempted measurements, all a little bit wrong. In this situation, if the measurement errors are **normally distributed** then the best estimate is the **least squares fitting** number.

But what if the measurement errors, or other data, are not **normally distributed**? It was noticed that sometimes even slight departures from **normality** made the **least squares fit** a poor choice.

The hunt was on for **estimators** that give a good estimate, in practice, even if the data are not **normally distributed**. These are called **robust estimators**.

More generally, robustness is a useful concept in risk mathematics. It refers to techniques that give reasonably good answers even when assumptions are not met very closely.

Data that don't match your assumptions are a problem for fitting data and a problem for evaluating **model uncertainty**.

139 OVER-FITTING

The fit between a **model** and the data used to establish its parameters is a rough guide to the accuracy of the predictions you can get from the **model**. However, it is not a reliable guide.

More often, the many parameters in a big **model** make it rather flexible, giving a good chance of fitting the **model** to past data. Generally, the more parameters you have, the more bendy the **model** and the better the fit.

The problem is that the **model** fits the past data precisely because it has been tweaked to do just that. It doesn't necessarily result in better predictions of new data. This is called **over-fitting**.

What we need to find is a good balance between simplicity and fit to past data. This usually gives superior predictions in future.

There have been attempts to say which is the best **model** given a choice between simple **models** and more bendy **models** that fit the data better. Typical of these is Akaike's information criterion, which penalizes **models** with lots of parameters.

140 DATA MINING

This is a broad term for data analysis that typically involves a massive number of data, very bendy **models**, and a lot of computerized number crunching. In particular, it tends to mean making predictions on the basis of a large number of other variables.

Popular techniques include generalized linear models, support vector machines, neural networks, Bayesian classifiers, genetic programming, and classification and regression trees, to name just some.

Sometimes it is possible to understand and analyse the performance of these techniques using the ideas described earlier in this book about **exhaustive, mutually exclusive hypotheses**. However, in many cases it is not and with neural networks in particular there is very little that can be analysed in traditional terms. They work, but it's hard to see why.

Of course the days when you needed a computer the size of a motor-home to do **data mining** are long gone and today's laptops can do astonishing things. The power is intoxicating, but don't get carried away!

With so many data almost any connection between variables, even a rather weak one, can be picked up and included in the **model**. With such flexible, multi-parameter **models** it is possible to take **over-fitting** to new highs. And with the computer checking for so many potentially important relationships it is almost inevitable that a lot of what it finds will be just coincidental.

141   AUDIT POINT: SEARCHING FOR 'SIGNIFICANCE'

In the entry about **hypothesis testing** we looked at techniques for estimating how likely some data are assuming a particular hypothesis is true. If the data would be extremely unlikely assuming a hypothesis then we can confidently reject the hypothesis. The **probabilities** coming out of these calculations assume that only one hypothesis test is done.

In practice it is very common to test *repeatedly* for a 'significant difference' and of course from time to time you will find one. To say that a difference is 'significant at the 5% level' means that on average as many as one in twenty sets of data will appear to be 'significant' in this sense, by sheer coincidence.

For example, if you are looking for unusual error rates in processing commodity trades and there are 124 types of trade to check then clearly some of those are likely to appear significantly different from the others, even when they aren't.

Most **data mining** techniques involve so many parameters and examination of so many potentially interesting relationships that **hypothesis testing** is totally impractical.

Two mistakes are possible. One is to think that 'significant' really is significant despite the extensive searching. The other is to think that 'significant' is totally meaningless and that a 'significant' item is no more likely to be interesting than any other.

142 EXPLORATORY DATA ANALYSIS

Don't give up on **data mining**. **Exploratory data analysis (EDA)** is analysis that involves a range of techniques for searching data sets looking for interesting patterns that may turn out to have interesting explanations.

EDA was pioneered by statistician and all-round brainy person John Tukey (1915–2000) in the days when computers were not available to help. His clever graphs and quick analysis tricks are a delight and I think he would have loved playing with today's computers.

Data mining is like a modern version of **EDA** that uses computer power to explore more quickly.

The value of **EDA** is that the apparent connections it finds are more likely to be real than other connections. The problem is that we don't have much idea *how likely* they are to be real.

143 CONFIRMATORY DATA ANALYSIS

Once **exploratory data analysis** (or **data mining**) has found some interesting relationships the next stage, ideally, is to study more rigorously to see if they are real or just coincidence. This is sometimes called **confirmatory data analysis**.

144 INTERPOLATION AND EXTRAPOLATION

When a **model** is created and fit to existing data it can be used to try to predict new data in two ways. If it is used to predict data *inside* the range covered by the data used to fit it then that is **interpolation**. If it is used to predict data *outside* the range covered by the data used to fit it then that is **extrapolation**.

Since most **models** are fit to past data and used to predict future data they are **extrapolating**.

For obvious reasons, **interpolating** is more likely to be successful than **extrapolating**.

145   AUDIT POINT: SILLY EXTRAPOLATION

There's nothing wrong, in principle, with **extrapolation**. We have to do it and it's better than just guessing, usually.

The problem comes when we **extrapolate** in circumstances where it should be obvious that the new data will be systematically different from past data used to fit the **model**.

The credit crunch of 2007–2009 was helped on its way by two examples of silly **extrapolation**. At the root of this crisis were optimistic assessments of the risk of home buyers failing to keep up with mortgage repayments.

Analysts thought that, because default rates across the USA had not correlated strongly in the past, they wouldn't in the future. However, as house prices fell across the entire country the correlations soared. Something had changed – the trend in house prices – and that had made **extrapolation** unsafe. (To be more precise, they thought the correlations were **normally distributed** but in fact, once again, the tails were fatter than **normal**.)

Analysts also thought that, because default rates in the past had been fine, even on the rare occasions when full documentation had not been obtained to confirm things like income, this would continue to be the case in future, even if documentation-free loans were strongly marketed. In fact offering mortgages in this way invited fraud and stupid risk taking.

In this case, acting on the **extrapolation** actually changed the behaviour of the **system** to such an extent that **extrapolation** was unsafe.

146 CROSS VALIDATION

The astonishing number crunching muscle of today's ordinary laptop makes possible a simple way of assessing the fit of a **model** to data that partially guards against **over-fitting**.

The method is to split your available data into two sets. One of those sets is used for **model fitting** and is called the training data set. The other is used for validation and is called the validation data set.

Once the **model** has been fitted to the training data set its fit to the validation data set is calculated. Usually the fit is worse for the validation data set, and this drop gives an idea of just how much **over-fitting** has occurred.

To get a more reliable assessment, this **cross validation** is usually done a number of times, splitting the full data set differently each time, and averaging the results.

147 R² (THE COEFFICIENT OF DETERMINATION)

A very common way to express how well a **model** fits or predicts some data is by calculating the R^2, pronounced 'R squared'.

R^2 ranges from zero to one and higher numbers are better. R^2 is often given as a number representing the percentage of **variance** 'accounted for' by a model. For example, an R^2 of 0.94 means that 94% of the **variance** is 'accounted for' by the **model**.

R^2 is the square of the **linear correlation** between a set of data points and predictions for those data points produced by a **model**.

Linear correlation is generally accepted as a measure of how closely linked two variables are, just as R^2 is widely used and generally accepted.

However, there are some problems to be aware of and in general it makes sense to inspect graphs of predictions and actuals before drawing any conclusions.

The first problem arises because the **linear correlation** only recognizes linear links between pairs of variables, i.e. if they were shown on a graph it would be a straight line. It would be quite possible for a **model** to make predictions that closely tracked reality but were not linear. These would still be poor predictions, but on a graph you would be able to see that the **model** was doing a promising job and a bit of tweaking could produce good predictions.

The second problem arises because R^2 reflects the **correlation** between actuals and predictions, not the accuracy of the predictions. If the predictions were always, say, half the actuals then they would have a great R^2 even though they were consistently wrong. The same problem arises if the predictions are different from the actuals by the same amount each time.

The third problem is an extension of the second and is the result of R^2 being the *square* of the **correlation**. If the **correlation** is negative, because the predictions are rising as the actuals decline, this does not detract from the R^2 score.

The fourth problem is the one I've been plagued by most in practice. When you inspect the graph of data points to see how your predictions matched up to reality what you often see is a tightly packed bundle of data points in one place, and then a solitary data point lying a long way from the main group. The R^2 thinks this is quite persuasive evidence of good predictions.

Incidentally, there are alternative measures of links between variables, including 'mutual information', which does not require a linear relationship.

148   AUDIT POINT: HAPPY HISTORY

The data chosen for **model** fitting and validation can be crucial to overall predictive reliability. For example, some banks have been caught out by basing their **models** on periods of financial history in which nothing remarkable happened.

Unfortunately, remarkable things happen from time to time in financial markets and you only have to go back far enough to find them.

More generally, people tend to gather more data, and more consistently, during periods without much turmoil, with obvious dangers for modellers.

149   AUDIT POINT: SPURIOUS REGRESSION RESULTS

Imagine we are trying to predict one variable and have values for dozens of other variables that might be predictors of it. One technique that aims to seek out those variables that are the best predictors is called stepwise regression.

Stepwise regression can be done in various ways but they all involve trying lots of combinations of variables to see if they are predictive, and trying to boil it down to a small set of variables that, together, are highly predictive.

Variables that are selected for inclusion in this way are more likely to be genuinely predictive than variables discarded by the procedure. However, in data sets with no real relationships at all, stepwise regression will often find what appear to be strong predictive relationships and will even report that they are highly significant statistically.

Clearly, **models** developed using this method need to be treated with caution.

150   INFORMATION GRAPHICS

Often the best, most convincing way to see if data tell a useful story is to look at the right graph. This could be a graph that just shows the data or one that shows the data and predictions by a **model**.

Information graphics are vital to understand data. They should be high resolution, rich in detail, beautifully refined, and focus their space and ink on showing as much information as possible.

151   AUDIT POINT: DEFINITION OF MEASUREMENTS

Sometimes fitting a **model** to data is easy — just some clicks on a computer — and yet still the results are fatally flawed. A common reason for this is that one or more of the data fields used does not represent what it is thought to represent.

It is depressing how often it is impossible to establish definitely what a field in a database represents. Sometimes there is no documentation at all. More often the available description is vague or ambiguous. Occasionally the definition has changed during the period whose data the analyst wants to use.

Sometimes the problem is that the method of measurement involves an unrecognized element of smoothing. For example, calls received by a call centre are not evenly spread over time. There are peaks and understanding how high those peaks are might be very important to someone planning staffing or equipment for a call centre. But what if the only data available are past hourly call volumes? An unremarkable hour might still include a devastating two minute flood.

A similar issue might arise for wind speed, rainfall, wave heights, website hits, and security breaches.

Auditors should look very hard at the issue of data definitions. In my experience it is as common as significant data errors and can cause bigger mistakes.

152 CAUSATION

Correlation does not prove **causation**. For example, suppose a sports coach angrily berates his players after a poor performance and praises them after a good one. Looking back, he notices that his angry ranting seems to be associated with better performances next time, while his praise seems to cause poorer performance next time. Obviously, giving the players a hard time works and praise is a waste of breath. It's a licence to bully.

Of course these data prove nothing of the sort. Performance fluctuates from one occasion to the next for lots of reasons. If one session goes particularly badly then the next will probably be better regardless of what the coach does. Conversely, if the session goes particularly well then it is likely that performance will be less good next time, again regardless of the coach.

Actually the familiar mantra that **correlation** does not prove **causation** is slightly misleading. **Correlation** is very good evidence that there is **causation** at work *somewhere*, but it doesn't tell us how. If X correlates with Y then most likely either X causes Y, or Y causes X, or something else causes both of them.

**Correlation
does not prove
causation**

To a limited extent, statistics can help us understand **causality** using only **correlations**, but it cannot establish a unique causal explanation unless it uses the timing differences between cause and effect to establish the direction of **causality**. Usually, all the statistics can do is rule out some explanations because they are inconsistent with the data.

Finally, let's go back to the friend of a friend with the betting system. He said:

> *I've found a way to make money by betting on the outcomes of league football matches. It's amazing. I've been number crunching*

Table 4 Ways to ignore uncertainty in modelling

Interpret probability purely as long run relative frequency, but do not explain this when presenting results

Assume extrapolation is safe

Assume the process is unchanging

Choose a model that ignores extremes

Ignore alternative models

Do not validate the choice of model

Accept a normality test with limited data

Ignore problems with the quality and definition of data used for fitting, cross validation, back-testing, and model inputs

Underplay correlations

Use estimators e.g. MLE, MAP

Use p values that ignore the effect of hunting for significance, e.g. from stepwise regression

---

through years of past results and by fitting a probit model using stepwise regression I've found some variables that predict results better than the bookmakers and they're highly significant statistically. And look, I've even done simulations showing that, if I'd used my system over the last few years, I would have made a healthy profit. Do you want to get in on the action?

Now can you see the potential problem? **Regression** naturally reminds us of the dangers of **over-fitting** and when we learn that he relied on **stepwise regression** alarm bells ring loudly. This is the method that can generate what it says is a statistically significant result from pure junk. The obvious check would be **cross validation** but he doesn't seem to have done any. Instead he did the simulation using the very same data his model was tuned to.

This imaginary example was inspired by a real research report I read. In the study the researcher *did* perform cross validation and it showed that the model did *not* in fact predict results any better than bookmakers. This should have stopped him in his tracks and yet it had no impact on his conclusions. As an auditor you need to understand that quants desperately want their models to be valuable and this can make them ignore unwelcome results.

AUDITING AND SAMPLES

Sampling is really just another topic within the general area of validating models. We've already looked at populations, fitting models to data, and at validation.

We're just going to take things a bit further because of the special place that sampling has in the life of auditors.

Don't skip this chapter, even if you feel a bit cynical about sampling.

And why would an auditor feel cynical about sampling? Where do I start?

When I was a novice auditor many years ago the right sample size was always 30, dropped from the old-fashioned 50. A sample size of 30 left you 95% confident of something-or-other. Over the years audit budgets were squeezed and squeezed and eventually the right sample size drifted down to more like 5, and even 3 if you had special reasons. Then along came the Sarbanes-Oxley Act, increased pressure for thoroughness, and new money. Hey presto, sample sizes jumped up to old-fashioned levels like 50 or more.

Justifications have generally been pseudo-statistical and perhaps careful to avoid being specific in case clarity made it possible to prove in court that an auditor had made a mistake.

A moment's spreadsheeting will tell you that being 95% confident on each of, say, 50 unrelated issues covered in an audit implies that you are just under 8% confident that none of the issues is present! Is 95% a good choice?

The point of understanding the real value of evidence is not usually to encourage heroic efforts to test giant samples. The main practical result is that we will want to make sure people understand just how little the evidence is telling them, and how much risk they still face.

This chapter is directly relevant to audit technique because, of course, auditors have to combine evidence and use samples. It is also relevant because auditors will sometimes have to review how others have used evidence, including evidence from samples.

153 SAMPLE

A couple of chapters ago we met the idea of a **population**, typically the output of some **process** or **system**. We noted that **models** can be of the **process** or of a **population**.

We have to make a choice between alternatives and it can involve some creativity

As with so many fundamental things in risk mathematics, **populations** do not define themselves. We have to make a choice between alternatives and it can involve some creativity. It's vital to make that choice, get it clear, and write it down.

A **sample** is a subset of a **population**. **Samples** can be selected in many different ways, and the best choice depends on what we want to learn.

154 AUDIT POINT: MIXED POPULATIONS

Some **populations** are a better choice than others. For example, a **population** of pigs might be a better choice than a **population** of pigs and chickens. The pigs and the chickens are so different from each other, and so obviously from two different groups, that it is hard to see what value there is in treating them together as one **population**.

With pigs and chickens it's obvious, but many situations where we use **populations** are complicated by the same issue, but it is *not* obvious.

155 ACCESSIBLE POPULATION

Sometimes the **population** we want to model is not entirely within reach. It may be that we are interested in all thefts from a large retailer, but most thefts go unnoticed. Sure, we know the stock has gone, but we don't know if that was because of one theft or more than one.

The **population** we are interested in is the theoretical **population**, but the **population** we can actually get access to is the **accessible population**.

156 SAMPLING FRAME

If we've defined our **population** and the **accessible population** within that, are we ready to draw a sample? No, not quite.

We need a **sampling frame**, which is a list of items from which to draw our sample, or a procedure that will serve the same purpose.

For example, if the theoretical **population** is customers of a particular company during a period of time, then the **accessible population** is typically the customers still in business at the address given to the company, and the **sampling frame** might be the customer database matched against sales during the period.

157 SAMPLING METHOD

Now can we draw a **sample**? No. We need to choose a **sampling method**.

The way we choose the **sample** depends on what we want to learn from it. For example, if we want to find suppliers that are cheating us then it makes sense to select suppliers for study that seem likely to be cheats. We would pick out certain features we think might be indicators of cheating and take a **sample** of suppliers having those features.

The most common goals of sampling ... are to estimate non-compliance rates and to estimate the value of errors

In another case we might want to know the average default rate on loans made by a bank in a particular town. For that we need to use a different **sampling method**.

The most common goals of sampling in audit work are to estimate non-compliance rates and to estimate the value of errors.

158 PROBABILITY SAMPLE (ALSO KNOWN AS A RANDOM SAMPLE)

A **probability sample** is one where the **sample** items were selected using some kind of **random** process (or **pseudo random**) so that the **probability** of selecting each item in the **sample** is known, and greater than zero.

That **probability** doesn't have to be the same for every item in the **sample**; it just has to be known. With this knowledge it is possible to weight each sample item to adjust for its chance of inclusion in the sample.

This kind of sampling is useful for estimating the average default rate on loans made by a bank in a particular town, and similar inferences. Done correctly it removes bias from the **sample**.

A lot of sampling theory is dedicated to estimating **means** and **variances** of **populations**, but remember that this is just an aspect of **model fitting** and validation using data, and our real interest might be the **process** generating the **population** rather than the **population** itself. Also we might be trying to develop a much more elaborate and interesting **model** than just one that summarizes a **population**.

159 EQUAL PROBABILITY SAMPLING (ALSO KNOWN AS SIMPLE RANDOM SAMPLING)

The most commonly mentioned type of **probability sampling** is where each item in the **sampling frame** is equally likely to be selected for the **sample**. This idea is so dominant you may have been surprised to learn that a **random sample** doesn't have to have this property.

Strictly speaking, for **equal probability sampling** it is not enough that each item in the **sampling frame** has an equal **probability** of inclusion. It is also necessary for every pair of items to have an equal **probability** of inclusion, and every triple, and so on.

Though simple in principle, **equal probability sampling** is not very efficient.

160 STRATIFIED SAMPLING

One tweak that usually squeezes more information from a given total **sample** size is to divide the **sampling frame** into subsets (known as strata) on the basis of a variable thought to **correlate** with whatever you are most interested in for the study. **Probability samples** are then drawn from each stratum.

Not only does this allow you to make inferences about each stratum individually, but it is also more efficient than treating the **sampling frame** as one **population** – meaning that you can draw firmer conclusions from a given number of **sample** items.

161 SYSTEMATIC SAMPLING

Another tweak that works on a similar basis is to sort the **sampling frame** on the basis of a variable thought to be linked to the objective of the study, then select every *kth* item for your **sample**, starting from a randomly selected initial item.

For example, if you have 100 items to sample from and want a **sample** of 5 then the procedure is to select a number from 1 to 20 inclusive at random, and use this as the starting item, then take every 20th item counting on from there.

This means that each item has an **equal probability** of being sampled, but it does not make every subset of the **sampling frame** equally like to be selected, which was the requirement for **equal probability sampling**.

162 PROBABILITY PROPORTIONAL TO SIZE SAMPLING

Another efficiency booster is to tune the **probability** of selecting each item for the **sample** to some measure of size.

The example that many auditors know is monetary unit sampling, which combines the idea of **systematic sampling** with **probability proportional to size sampling**.

163 CLUSTER SAMPLING

Sometimes travel costs are important, so a method of limiting these is to use **cluster sampling**. In this method the total geographical region from which the **sample** items are to be chosen is divided into areas.

Some areas are chosen at random, and then from within these areas a set of **sample** items is chosen.

The downside of these techniques for making sampling more efficient is that they require more complicated mathematical methods. Not surprisingly, software is usually the answer for most people.

There are many, many more **sampling methods** but it's time to move on.

164 SEQUENTIAL SAMPLING

Having chosen a **sampling method**, now can we draw a **sample**? No. We need to decide how many items to **sample**. However, that doesn't mean we have to decide the *total* number of items we will **sample**.

A really smart approach is item-by-item **sequential sampling**, where we have a **sample** size of one, draw that **sample**, analyse the evidence, draw another **sample** of one, analyse the evidence, and so on until we are content to stop. The analysis can often be done instantly by spreadsheet software and simple formulae, especially where **conjugate distributions** can be used.

Typically, people end up testing bigger samples than necessary

An alternative form is group **sequential sampling**, where we choose a small **sample** size and select repeated **samples**, each time evaluating the evidence so far, and stopping when content.

The more familiar approach of committing in advance to a total **sample** size and drawing it just once is a bit of a gamble. You don't know if you will be content with the results or not, and if you want to be sure you have to pick a bigger **sample** size than you will probably need. Typically, people end up testing bigger **samples** than necessary when they commit in advance.

165   AUDIT POINT: PREJUDGING SAMPLE SIZES

A lot of people think that total **sample** sizes can and should be established before evidence is gathered. It is true that having some idea of what is likely to be a worthwhile total **sample** size is important for practical reasons, but it is rarely true that the required total **sample** size can be established up front.

In reality the number of items needed to make some given inference usually depends on what the data show.

For example, if the objective is to be 95% confident that the error rate in some **process** is less than 1% then the number of items needed in the **sample** depends on:

- the actual error rate from the process; and
- the errors that happen to be found in the **sample**.

Imagine that the actual error rate is just a little below 1%. In this case a huge number of items will usually need to be tested to be 95% confident that the error rate is indeed below 1%.

If the actual error rate is well above 1% then clearly no sample size, no matter how large, is going to do the job!

And here's another example. Suppose the objective is to estimate some number using a **sample** so that you are 90% confident that the actual value lies within 5% of the estimate, above and below.

In this case the number of **sample** items required depends on how variable the data in the **sample** are. Imagine that all the items selected for the **sample** had the same value. That should leave you more confident that you know where the true average is than you would be if the data in your **sample** were wildly different from each other.

If that imaginary example didn't convince you then take a look at **sample** sizing techniques for this kind of inference and you will see a step where it asks for an estimate of the variability of the **population**. As if you would know this without having studied the data!

In general, the smaller the effects or differences we want to study and the more variable the data, the larger the **sample** has to be. Neither of those things is known to us until we start looking at data.

If someone is acting like they think they can fix the total **sample** size in advance then either they are probably making a mistake or they are prepared to accept whatever degree of confidence the data will provide.

166 DROPOUTS

Now can we draw a **sample**? Yes! And are these the items we're including in our study? Yes. And whose data we use? No.

No, because some items selected for the **sample** may not give you data you can use. Perhaps you wanted to interview a **sample** of people but some refused to participate, or refused to answer certain questions. **Dropouts** are a major reason for **samples** being biased.

Dropouts are a major reason for samples being biased

167 AUDIT POINT: SMALL POPULATIONS

The smaller the **population**, the more we should worry about two problems that render the usual textbook formulae increasingly inaccurate.

A lot of statistical formulae assume that the **population** is infinitely large, which makes the formulae much simpler than they otherwise would be. Obviously, infinitely large **populations** don't really exist at all but there is a more practical way of looking at this.

Suppose an accounts clerk processed 9 large, complex invoices during a year. The clerk's work is a **process** that generates the occasional error. An *internal* auditor, for example, could look at the 9 invoices as evidence of that tendency to produce errors and report on it. This might be useful information about future work by the clerk.

The mathematician sees this tendency to produce errors as a parameter of an infinite **population** of invoices by the clerk including all past and future possible invoices, and then some. I think it is easier and more logical to think of this as modelling the properties of the **process**.

An *external* auditor, in contrast, might be most interested in the 9 invoices themselves because they are included in the accounts for a year and the auditor wants to know if the accounts are right. The mathematician sees that as involving a finite **population** of just 9 items.

If it had been 9,000 invoices then the difference between estimating **process** properties and **population** properties is small numerically. At just 9 invoices it is an important factor.

If we are interested in the properties of the **population**, and the **population** is smallish, then it matters if we sample with or without replacement. Let me explain.

The usual way to select a **sample** is to choose items one by one in such a way that if an item has been chosen it is not eligible to be chosen again. This is called sampling without replacement. Intuitively this makes sense. If we replace items after sampling them then they can be sampled again.

Sampling without replacement is a problem for many statistical formulae because it means that later **sample** items are not independent of earlier ones.

However, since the **population** is usually assumed to be infinitely large it doesn't matter if we replace items or not because the chance of picking the same one twice is zero. The dependency vanishes.

In contrast, with a small **population** and a largish **sample** the inaccuracies can become important.

Going back to our example of the accounts clerk who raises 9 invoices in a year, the internal auditor's estimate of **process** properties will be hampered by having only 9 invoices as evidence. In contrast, the external auditor's estimate of **population** properties will be perfect if all 9 invoices are checked and probably good enough if a fairly high proportion have been checked.

Although the justifications are complicated, fairly simple formulae exist to adjust for finite **populations**, and Bayesian methods can also accommodate this complication.

AUDITING IN THE WORLD OF HIGH FINANCE

Some of the most sophisticated, confusing, and highly remunerated risk mathematics is done in the world of high finance. Brilliant minds try to squeeze out advantages for big banks that invest in shares, commodities, currencies, derivatives, and other, more exotic, instruments. Insurance companies rely on the high priests of quantitative risk analysis, the actuaries.

Models are built to guide investment, to decide what is a good price for a security, to set the price of insurance, to decide the reserves an insurance company needs, and to decide the capital a bank should have.

This is very clever stuff by very clever people, backed by staggering amounts of money. Does that mean it is right?

In hindsight we know the answer to that question is a resounding 'No!' Being rich does not necessarily make a person right, even if the money makes them very sure of themselves.

In some ways, the very power of this modelling is a danger, because it tempts people to believe that they can control their risks with the right deals and do things that in the past would have seemed too scary.

Model uncertainty is one of the big areas where improvements are needed. For example, if you are a trustee of a final salary pension fund in the UK you may have seen reports by actuaries to the scheme analysing how much money might be needed to pay for future pensions. This is a tricky thing to estimate and depends on how the economy progresses and how long pensioners live. A typical report contains one answer based on a table of assumptions made on a 'best estimate' basis, and another (different) answer made on the basis of legally required assumptions. There is virtually no information about model uncertainty, though there should be some comment about sensitivity to the most critical assumptions.

Most of the concepts of risk mathematics that you need to understand to audit in this high-powered world have already been covered in previous chapters of this book. In this chapter we will see how they apply.

168   EXTREME VALUES

A lot of attention in recent years has been devoted to understanding extreme events, such as market crashes and extreme weather.

In finance, it has been recognized that these do not fit the **normal distribution** very well. The problem is that unusual events happen too often.

A lot of attention in recent years has been devoted to understanding extreme events

Most early methods for calculating **value at risk (VaR)** assumed that returns were **normally distributed** and indeed this did fit the data very well, overall. However, the good fit in the central region of the distribution, where most of the available data are, masked the poor fit in the tails, where there are few data to ring alarm bells. Another problem is that **VaR** has little to say about losses beyond the **VaR** level.

Extreme value theory is an attempt to overcome these problems. First, it usually ignores all outcomes except the extreme ones, which emphasizes the problems with fitting the **normal distribution**, among others. Second, it argues that extreme events, by their very nature, have characteristic distributions.

You may remember that one of the reasons the **normal distribution** is so popular is that, in theory, the *sum* of the values returned by many **random variables** will be **normally distributed**, regardless of their distributions.

In a similar spirit, **extreme value** theorists have shown that the *maximum* (or minimum) of values returned by many, many **random**

variables, regardless of their distributions, will conform to the generalized extreme value distribution. Also, the distribution of losses beyond a threshold tends towards being a generalized Pareto distribution.

VaR modelling today is more likely to use some kind of **extreme value** theorizing to model the tails more accurately. It is also increasingly common to state the conditional **VaR** too, which is the **mean** of the tail beyond the **VaR** level. That gives at least some idea of how bad things could get.

However, all these distributions cling on to the assumption that more extreme events remain less likely. Another theory is that the distribution of losses could be bimodal, i.e. in addition to the main peak of the distribution there is another mini-peak in the extreme tail. In a financial market the idea is that this could be caused by a 'liquidity black hole' where selling precipitates more selling, leading to a rapid downward spiral and arrival at a new, somewhat stable state. It's as if the market is winded by a painful blow and has to sit down for a while to get its breath back.

169 STRESS TESTING

Another approach to dealing with the problem of **models** that only work in normal times is to imagine extreme scenarios and see what effect they would have. **Models** that do this can also be used to see the effect of an extreme event from history repeating.

City regulators strongly urge banks and insurance companies to do this kind of **stress testing**. On the plus side it gets more people involved in the modelling and opens up thinking to new possibilities. On the minus side it doesn't usually give **probability** numbers, though it could. City **models** tend to interpret **probability** in terms of **long run relative frequency** and ignore uncertainty about the **LRRF**. There is no logical reason why **probability** should not be used in **stress testing** provided the interpretations are clear.

170 PORTFOLIO MODELS

Models of portfolios of investments in shares, bonds, currencies, derivatives, etc. are used for a number of purposes but we are interested in their role in risk management. Here **portfolio models** are used to calculate **value at risk** and the amount of capital an institution should have to keep the chances of being ruined below some specified level.

For this purpose what is needed is a **probability distribution** for the value of the portfolio a certain number of days from now. How many days ahead this looks depends on various factors, including how often the content of the portfolio is changed, but could be anywhere between one day (typical) and one year (less typical).

In ordinary language the phrase 'risk factor' usually means something that is true ... that drives risk in some way

The early attempts to do this started by modelling the prices of individual shares, usually by fitting a **normal distribution** to past share price movements. These **models** were combined into one **normal distribution** for the whole portfolio by taking into account how many of each share was in the portfolio and the **correlations** between the prices of every pair of shares.

For simple cases there is a **closed form** expression that gives the **standard deviation** of the portfolio distribution given the **standard deviations** of all the distributions of individual share prices and all the **correlations**. An alternative is to use **Monte Carlo simulation** to combine the distributions, though this gets harder the more different shares you have.

The more modern approach introduces a new idea called a 'risk factor'. Risk factors include the prices of shares and bonds, currency exchange rates, commodity prices, and interest rates. Typically, the number of risk factors that have to be modelled is much less than the number of different securities, which is why this technique is used.

(In ordinary language the phrase 'risk factor' usually means something that is true, or at least fairly certain, that drives risk in some way. However, in the world of **VaR** modelling, risk factors are the crucial unknowns.)

The movements of risk factors are modelled individually and combined in some way, such as with **correlations** or **copulas**.

The risk factor movements produced by the **models** are translated into portfolio value movements to produce the portfolio **probability distribution** that is the object of the exercise. The translation is based on understanding something called the 'portfolio mapping function'.

This portfolio mapping function has two key stages: (1) working out prices for each type of security in the portfolio, given values of all the risk factors, using 'valuation functions', and (2) working out the total price of the portfolio by adding up the individual securities.

The valuation function that gives the price of a share is ridiculously simple: the risk factor is the price of the share and the value is the same number. You may be wondering what the risk factors contribute to this exercise.

However, imagine the price of the share is in a foreign currency. Now the valuation function is the price of the share translated into the home currency using another risk factor, an exchange rate. Things get much more complicated with derivatives, where their prices can be estimated fairly accurately given half a dozen or so risk factors.

So, to summarize, the approach has to combine (1) a **probabilistic model** of how the risk factors move (together), with (2) the deterministic portfolio mapping function that turns particular values for the risk factors into a valuation of the portfolio. Given these two it has to produce a **probability distribution** for the portfolio's overall value.

171 HISTORICAL SIMULATION

Modelling the movements of individual risk factors is hard enough, but easy compared to trying to capture the way they move together. **Correlations** only express one type of link between variables and can easily miss important links, leading to an underestimate of **risk**.

Historical simulation ducks out of the hard work of trying to model all this by making the sweeping assumption that the immediate future will be just like the past.

The calculations for a 1-day **VaR** begin with data on the risk factors for a past period, usually something like two years. For each trading day in that past period the movement in the risk factors is applied to the current risk factor values and current portfolio to calculate a total value for the portfolio one day from now. So we get from this a list of the days in the history and against each day is a value for the whole current portfolio in one day's time.

A **value at risk** can be calculated from this either by fitting some parametric curve to these prices or by putting the days in ascending value order and reading off the values of particular days. For example, if you used 500 days of history and want the 5% **VaR** then that means you will take a day about 26 up from the lowest value.

Although **historical simulation** is easy to do and can pick up complex interdependencies between risk factors, it has its weaknesses. One is that it does not include things that have not happened in the historical period used.

172 HETEROSKEDASTICITY

If you can say **heteroskedasticity** after a few drinks then you're definitely starting to show some confidence with risk mathematics! (Read it carefully and say it to yourself a few times to make sure you pick up all eight syllables.)

historical simulation ... assumes that tomorrow will be just like the last few hundred days

Graphs of share prices show how they go through periods of relative stability where prices do not move much each day and then other periods of higher volatility where the prices move much more. This changing **variance** of movements is called **heteroskedasticity**.

The **historical simulation** approach doesn't take this into account. It assumes that tomorrow will be just like the last few hundred days. On days when everyone knows the markets are in turmoil this seems a particularly odd assumption.

173 RISKMETRICS VARIANCE MODEL

An alternative popularized by the influential RiskMetrics group is to track the **variance** of a risk factor over time and try to predict it. Their early methods for doing this included using the average **variance** of daily changes over the previous year and using an exponentially weighted **moving average** of recent changes that gave more weight to recent history than to older history.

In the initial methodology they still assumed that the daily changes were **normally distributed**, but the **variance** of that distribution changed over time, so that the distribution of price movements over a longer period had much fatter tails.

Compared to the **historical simulation** approach this should give **probabilities** that have greater **resolution**.

174 PARAMETRIC PORTFOLIO MODEL

With techniques like this it is possible to model the movements of individual risk factors more closely using parametric distributions. Combining these with parameters representing the **correlations** between risk factors gives enough information to use **Monte Carlo simulation** to reach the required **probability distribution** for portfolio value.

Alternatively, if the valuation functions are simple enough (i.e. so long as you don't hold derivatives and some other non-linear things) there is a **closed form** expression that allows a computer to calculate the **standard deviation** of the **probability distribution** of the portfolio's value almost instantly. If you then assume that the portfolio's **probability distribution** has a particular type (e.g. it is **normally distributed**) then you can calculate the **VaR** numbers.

175 BACK-TESTING

This is the general name for trying out a strategy or **model** using historical data to see what would have happened if you had used it during that past period.

Applied to **portfolio models** used to calculate **value at risk** this tends to focus on **calibration**. As a reminder of the logic involved, if you calculate 95%, 1-day **VaR**s for 100 days you would expect, on average, the actual loss to exceed the **VaR** for that day on 5 occasions. If it's a lot more or a lot less then that's evidence of poor **calibration**.

If actual losses exceed **VaR** too often then this increases the regulatory capital requirement under the Basel Accord.

A related test is to see if the frequency of losses exceeding the **VaR** is in any way affected by whether it happened the day before. This is called independence testing.

Don't forget that good **calibration** is only half the battle. We also want high **resolution**, something the City has not been so quick to realize. To some extent, independence testing is likely to pick up some of the issues that drive **resolution**, but it is still not a complete approach to judging the quality of **probabilities**.

Back-testing is the main way **model uncertainty** is understood in this type of modelling, but is limited to testing against historical data, so may not provide full information about **model uncertainty**.

176 AUDIT POINT: RISK AND REWARD

One of the pervasive ideas to come out of theories of financial markets is the belief that **risk** and reward are linked.

Specifically, a common assumption in theorizing is that if an investment seems more risky then investors will need more reward *in percentage terms* to tempt them to invest. Usually, they will achieve this by paying less for the investment but expecting the same rewards. In short, **risk** should drive prices down.

Unfortunately, this has been distorted in the popular imagination into the bizarre idea that **risk** and reward are always linked, not just in financial markets, so that taking more **risk** will *inevitably* result in making more money.

People are exhorted to be less **risk** averse, to thrive on **risk**, to see **risk** as positive, and so on. All this is nonsense. If we don't like an outcome then we also don't like the possibility of that outcome occurring. If a **risk** measure properly reflects this, as it should, then we don't like **risk**.

What is positive is the ability to think of less risky ways to do profitable things. It may also be possible to buy things at lower prices if you can show that the risk involved is greater than the seller would like you to believe. In short, managing **risk** is positive, but not **risk** itself.

177 PORTFOLIO EFFECT

There are two **portfolio effects**. The best known is the value of diversification. If you have £1 million to spend on shares, should you spend it all on shares of one company or spread your money around? If you are considering a number of shares with similar prospects it is best to spread your money around. The **probability distribution** of a diversified portfolio like this will have roughly the same average return as a typical share within the portfolio, but the spread of the return (and hence the chance of losing a lot of money) will be less than if you had spent it all on shares of one company.

That's the diversification effect, and it is stronger with lower **correlations** between the returns of the shares.

The other **portfolio effect** is volatility pumping. This arises because investors who own a portfolio of shares in different companies generally do so according to a policy that determines the composition of the portfolio. As share prices rise and fall they have to buy or sell shares to keep the portfolio roughly consistent with their policy.

Consequently, they systematically sell shares that have lost value (and are sometimes on their way down) and buy shares that have gained value (and are sometimes on their way up). This tends to improve returns.

178 HEDGE

Many techniques can be used as **hedges**. Confusingly, some definitions of the term in finance dictionaries actually equate **hedging** with particular techniques.

However, the idea is a general one and goes back to betting of all sorts, not just in the world of finance. The goal is to shape the **probability distributions** of future value or returns from your portfolio by making suitable agreements.

Many **hedging** techniques really do act like a boundary (think of a garden hedge) on losses, at least for elements within a portfolio. For example, buying a put option (the right to sell something at a pre-agreed price if you want to) does this because the worst that can happen is that you get the pre-agreed price.

In general, **hedging** individual holdings is less efficient than **hedging** bundles of less-than-fully-**correlated** holdings, if there is a way to do it.

Many hedging techniques really do act like a boundary (think of a garden hedge) on losses

179 BLACK–SCHOLES

Imagine you are trying to put in place an efficient **hedging** scheme for your portfolio and you're looking at various deals on offer, trying to decide what to do. Spotting good value for money is a major problem. What is the maximum you should pay for each type of deal?

In 1973, two economists, Fischer Black (1938–1995) and Myron Scholes (1941–), put forward a mathematical formula for pricing European call options, which are agreements allowing you to buy a particular quantity of a share at a particular price at a particular time, if you choose to. Their formula was based on the idea that the price of an option is related to the price of the share on which the option is based.

Robert C Merton (1944–), another economist, later published a paper generalizing the idea and giving it the name it bears today.

Merton and Scholes were awarded Nobel prizes for their contribution and Black probably only missed out because Nobel prizes are not given posthumously. Merton and Scholes are also famous for being directors of Long-Term Capital Management, a hedge fund that was wildly successful for four years before losing $4.6 billion in less than four months during 1998 by over-reliance on risk formulae.

Another worry is that mathematical explanations of formulae in this area are among the hardest to understand that you will find anywhere. This is probably a combination of the advanced techniques used and a cultural tendency not to bother with being completely clear. However, even if we can't follow the logic of the symbols we can at least get to grips with the assumptions made.

The **Black–Scholes** formula is a **closed form** solution to the **Black–Scholes** partial differential equation, which must be satisfied by the price of the derivative. This equation is derived from the **Black–Scholes model**, which is where all the assumptions are buried.

And what interesting assumptions they are. No commissions or taxes to pay, an efficient market, perfect liquidity so that instruments can be bought and sold in any quantity (even in infinitely small fractions of a unit) without delay or price drops, constant known risk-free interest rate, constant known volatility of the underlying share price, and of course **lognormal distribution** of share price movements.

By now you won't need me to tell you that all this adds up to a fantasy world where the inaccuracies of the formula are likely to increase the longer the time until the option is to be exercised.

In practice a lot of extra work is needed to compensate for the limitations of the formula.

Recently, Nicholas Taleb (of *Fooled by Randomness* and *Black Swans* fame) and Espen Haug have argued that the **Black–Scholes** formula is not, in fact, used widely as most people have assumed. Yes, traders may have software for it and may even use that software, but they fudge the volatility **input** to get the price they want, knowing that extreme price movements are more common than the **model** assumes. In many cases traders rely on market prices for options and something called the put-call parity rule, which allows them to infer prices of puts from calls and vice versa. On this basis, Taleb and Haug claim that the **Black–Scholes** formula isn't actually used at all in any meaningful sense.

Another problem with the **Black–Scholes** formula is that it is limited to very simple cases. As so often, to cope with real life we have to abandon neat formulae and boot up a computer.

The fastest calculation is with the **Black–Scholes** formula, but if the derivatives involved are a bit too complicated for that then the next step is to move to the binomial options pricing model.

This divides time into small steps up to the end of the option's life and then charts out a branching tree showing how the price of the underlying security could change in future. The software then works backwards through the tree rolling back the value of the option to the present moment.

This is a discrete approximation to the price and in terms of time, but is more flexible and accurate over longer periods because the assumptions can be slightly more realistic.

If this doesn't give enough flexibility, perhaps because multiple risk factors need to be taken into account (e.g. currency translation), then the next step is usually to move to **Monte Carlo simulation**. The **simulation** will take longer to execute and if seconds count then that can be a problem.

180 THE GREEKS

The price given by the **Black–Scholes** formula is sensitive to the inputs it is given. The terms of the option are known, but the interest rate and volatility have to be estimated (and assumed constant). Also, the current price and the time to expiry are always changing.

The rates at which the option's value changes (according to the formula) in response to changes in the various input values have been given names, mostly from the ancient Greek alphabet, and there are many more **Greeks** for rates of change of those rates of change, and so on.

For example, delta is the rate of change of the value of the option with changes in the current price of the underlying security. Theta shows the sensitivity of the value of the option to the passage of time. Vega is the rate of change of the value of the option with changes in volatility of the underlying security.

The idea behind the **Greeks** can also be applied to other investments and whole portfolios.

181   LOSS DISTRIBUTIONS

One common way to combine the frequency and severity distributions is using Monte Carlo simulation

One modelling technique often used for understanding events that lead to losses is to create a separate **model** for the frequency of the losses and another for their severity, then combine the two to create a **probability distribution** for losses over a period of time. This is often used in insurance and for modelling operational risk.

One common way to combine the frequency and severity distributions is using **Monte Carlo simulation**. On each of the thousands of simulation runs the computer first uses the frequency distribution to choose, pseudo randomly, a number of loss incidents. It then chooses pseudo random losses for each of those incidents using the severity distribution. Finally, it adds up the losses across the events to find the total loss. The accumulated results from thousands of these simulations build up the aggregate loss distribution, which is simply a **probability distribution** for the total loss in a specified period of time.

In practice, each type of risk event is usually modelled separately.

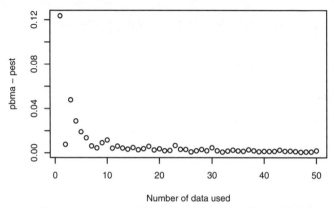

Figure 21 Difference between **Bayesian model averaging** and a best estimate (**MLE** basis) for the probability of more than 10 events using a **Poisson distribution**

The obvious distribution to assume for the frequency **model** is the **Poisson distribution** and a common method of fitting to data is to use the **maximum likelihood** basis. Figure 21 is much like Figure 19 and was created in a similar way. It shows how **Bayesian model averaging**, which reflects current uncertainty about **model** parameters rather than just picking the best guess, gives a more cautious assessment of the chance of more than twice the average number of events in one period.

With only one distribution parameter the difference seems to disappear quickly, but remember that the quant may only have a very few periods of historical data to work with, not 50.

Furthermore, all this is on the convenient assumption that the frequency distribution is not changing over time. In reality it is, so the true position is even less certain than the **model** may be saying, however you fit it.

182   AUDIT POINT: OPERATIONAL LOSS DATA

One of the big problems with using any approach to modelling operational risk is that data on past operational losses tend to be incomplete. Banks, the businesses that have done most in this area, have tended to rely on databases of past incidents that are populated in a spectacularly unreliable way. What is supposed to happen is that people should recognize an operational risk event has occurred, fill in a form, and go through a bureaucratic process to get the event valued and entered on the database.

As you can imagine, many smaller operational losses are not reported because people have better things to do with their time, values for recent events are often missing (because the debate about their value is still going on), operational risk events that give rise to gains are not usually reported at all even though they do sometimes happen, and the values of some events are unreliable. The frequency of events recorded can be driven strongly by the intensity of reminders people have been given to report incidents, so modelling tends to concentrate on losses over a specified threshold.

Many organizations try to classify the events according to their cause. While this is obviously a desirable goal it is often difficult to do it meaningfully and consistently. When many factors contribute to an incident the choice of which codes to apply on the database becomes rather subjective. For example, if someone thinks that training in their bank is very poor then they will tend to see evidence of that in most incidents. More generally, people have different preferences between blaming the individual and blaming the organization.

It is also common to classify events according to their type and doing this consistently is obviously important to modelling, especially when external databases are to be used to supplement data collected inside the organization. Unfortunately, the classification scheme suggested by the Basel II Accord is desperately vague, with many apparent overlaps and no sense of being a rigorous partition. A number of people have poked holes in it. To give you a flavour of the fun that can be had, its category for 'internal fraud' contains a sub-category named 'unauthorized behaviour', apparently implying that other fraud is authorized! Work has been done by various groups to offer more meaningful alternative classification schemes but progress is difficult. The Basel II scheme tends to dominate thinking and there are inherent difficulties in classifying events with so many contributing causes and resulting effects, particularly when the overall risk category itself has such fuzzy boundaries.

The key point for auditors is to expect problems with operational loss event data.

183   GENERALIZED LINEAR MODELS

A lot of **regressions** by actuaries use methods from a big toolkit called **generalized linear models**.

The sophisticated view of **regression**, you may remember, is that it involves creating a **probability distribution** for the variable(s) to be predicted that varies with one or more other variables used as predictors.

Generalized linear models have five elements:

- A 'distribution function' chosen from a particular set of **probability distributions** known as the exponential family (which includes the **normal distribution**, **binomial distribution**, and others). This is the curve that will give the shape of the prediction, but it needs its parameter values to be set. The parameters are its **mean** and **variance**.

- A set of predictor variables that provide the raw data from which a prediction might be made. For example, the cost of a driver's insurance claims might well be related to the driver's age, sex, past history of claims, and the value of the car driven. These would be important predictors.

- A set of weights to apply to each predictor variable. These weights are the key parameters in the **model** and finding good values for them usually involves running computer software.

- A 'link function' that takes as input the total value of all the predictor variables multiplied by their weights and returns as output a **mean** for the distribution function.
- A 'variance function' that works out a value for the **variance** of the distribution function, usually as a function of its **mean**.

At the heart of **generalized linear models** is the idea that what you are trying to predict is related in a straight line way to the predictors, but perhaps only after some adjustment by the link function.

An example of a **generalized linear model** is the general linear model. (Read that carefully!) In the general linear model several predictor variables are multiplied by weights (as usual) but the link function does nothing. It leaves the total unchanged. The distribution function is **normal** and its **variance** is often held constant.

CONGRATULATIONS

If you've read this far then you deserve to reward yourself. Your knowledge of risk mathematics – you perhaps prefer to talk about probability now – has mushroomed.

Of course there are still thousands of things you do not know and your understanding is only conceptual. You cannot actually perform the calculations on the basis of what is explained in this book.

However, your conceptual understanding may be better than that of some of the quants you might audit. They may be hazy about the interpretation of probability, unaware that there is more to back-testing than calibration, sceptical about Bayesian methods, and surprised that there are alternatives to using a best estimate.

Certain weaknesses are very common in applications of mathematics to 'risk' and the harder you look for them, the more you will find:

- Poor explanations, often written with breezy confidence, or in a baffling academic style, more effective at suppressing resistance than sharing knowledge.
- Convenient assumptions made then buried and forgotten, putting faith entirely in validation against actual data, but forgetting that this is always limited to past experience or still to be done.
- Best guess predictions based on elaborate models which in turn are based on pages of assumptions.
- Overlooking uncertainty about long run relative frequencies, leading to systematic overconfidence in models that passes unnoticed by almost everyone.
- Preference for normal distributions, maximum likelihood estimators, and other techniques that tend to cause systematic overconfidence, especially with complex models and limited data.

Good luck in your auditing!

APPENDIX

USEFUL WEBSITES

In general the *quantity* of information about risk mathematics freely available on the web is astonishing. If only it was all easy to understand.

Certain sources stand out as particularly informative or easy to work with.

- The NIST/Sematech *Engineering Statistics Handbook* is a model of clarity. Find it at: www.itl.nist.gov/div898/handbook/
- Glyn Holton's risk glossary is also outstanding. It's here: www.risk-glossary.com/
- Obviously Wikipedia is unavoidable because of its huge coverage, though some entries are hard to understand. To go direct use: www.wikipedia.org/

The various key phrases introduced in this book will usually produce lots of results if typed into Google or another search engine.

INDEX

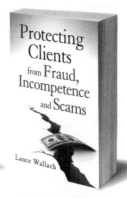

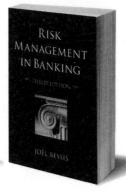

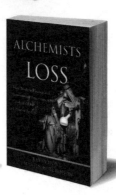